To Allan

Christmas 2020

Best Wishes

from Denise & Gordon

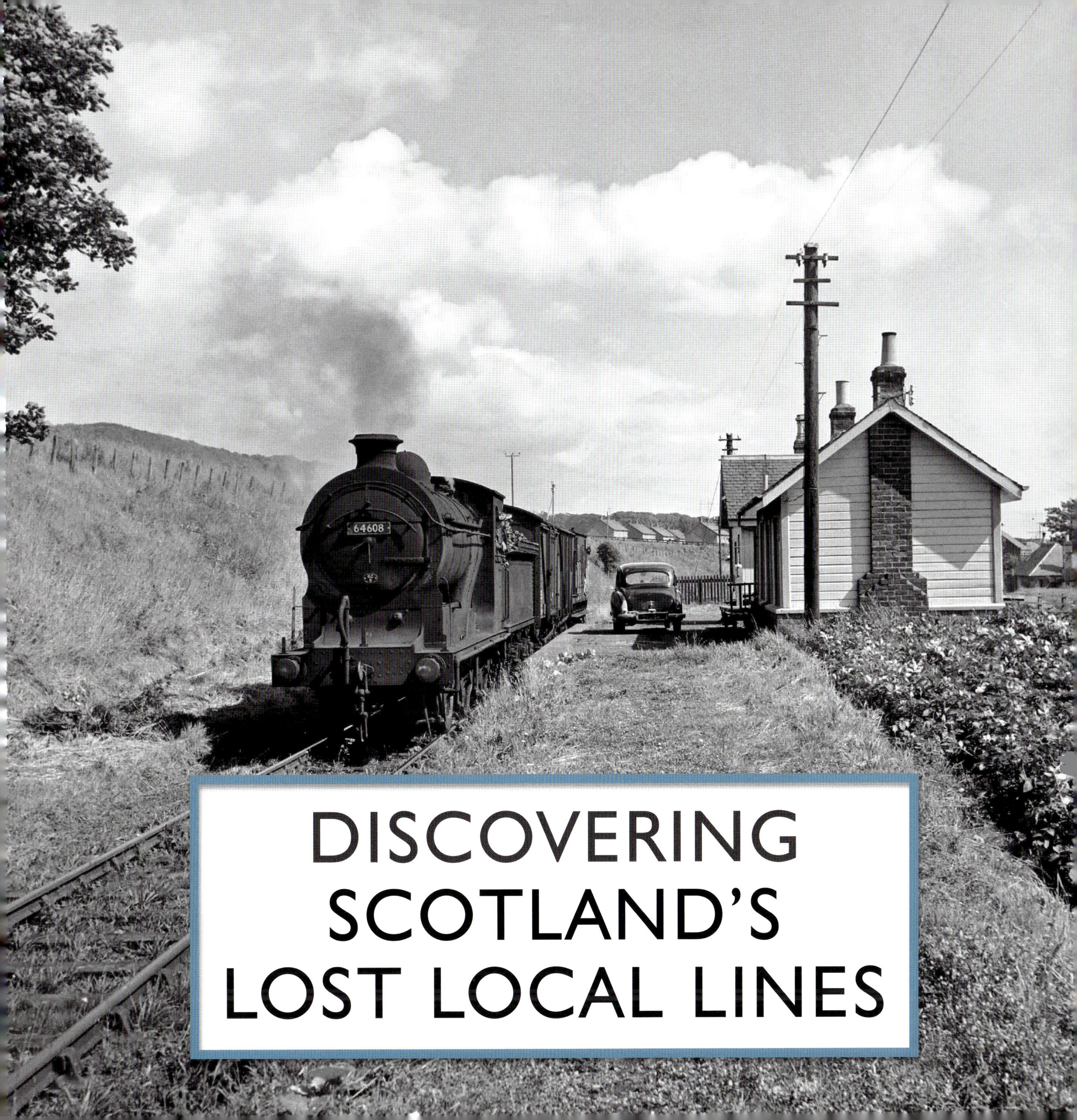

DISCOVERING SCOTLAND'S LOST LOCAL LINES

Previous page: *Ex-NBR Class J37 0-6-0 No. 64608 pauses at Johnshaven station with the daily freight train from Bervie (renamed Inberbervie in 1926) to Montrose on 5 August 1965. Steam-hauled to the end, the Bervie branch finally closed just over nine months later.*
This page: *The railway approach, behind the sea wall in the foreground, to the fishing village of Gourdon on the former Montrose to Bervie branch.*
Contents: *Ex-Highland Railway 'Ben' Class 4-4-0 No. 14398 'Ben Alder' is seen running round its train at Strathpeffer on 18 May 1928. The loco was later scheduled for preservation by British Railways but was mysteriously scrapped after being stored for years at various locations around Scotland. In the distance is Sentinel steam railcar No. 4149.*
Introduction: *Leaderfoot Viaduct once carried the Reston to St Boswells line across the River Tweed north of the latter town. The 19-arch viaduct is designated a Grade A listed structure.*

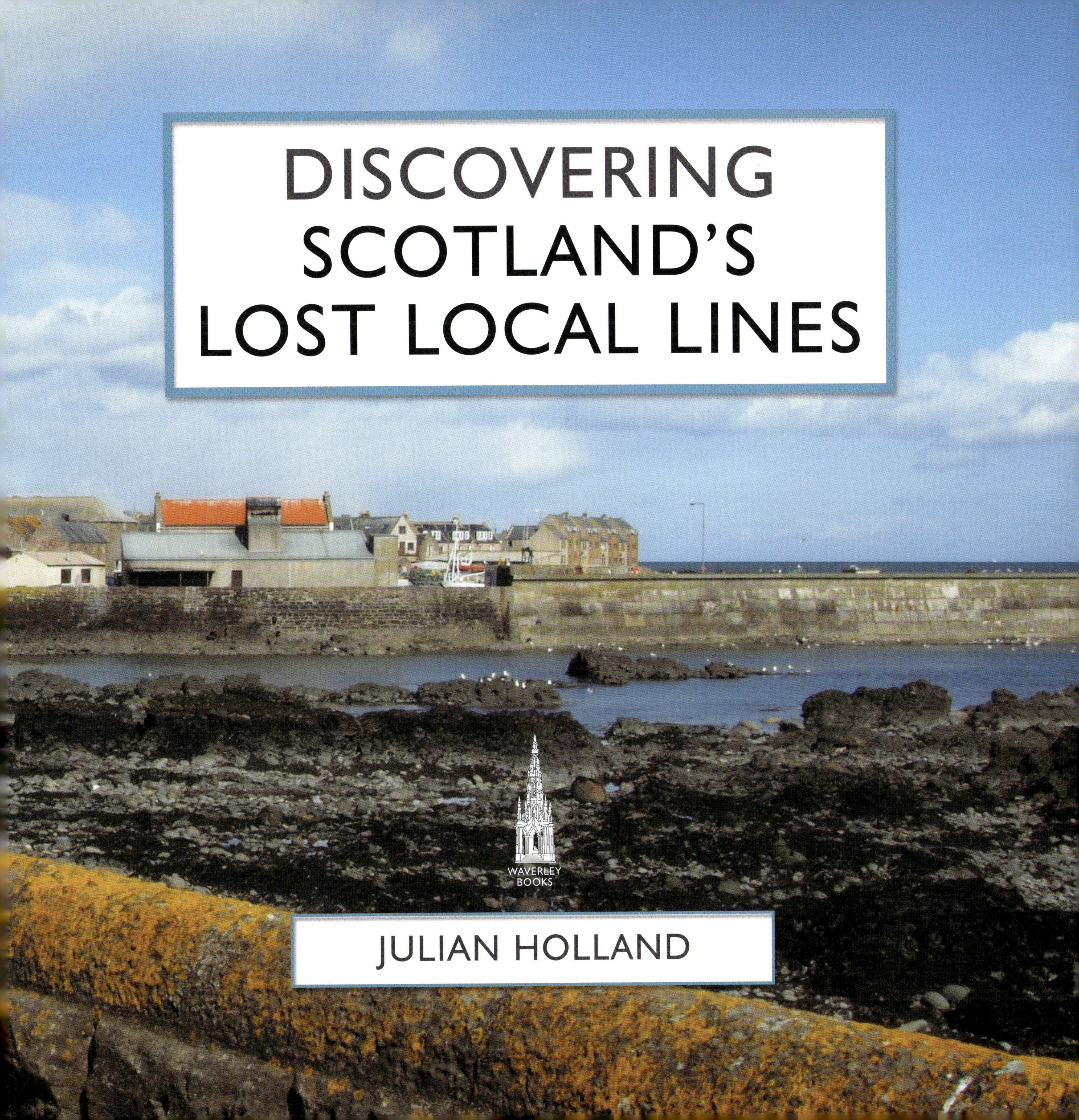
DISCOVERING
SCOTLAND'S
LOST LOCAL LINES
WAVERLEY
BOOKS
JULIAN HOLLAND

Published 2010 by Waverley Books,
144 Port Dundas Road, Glasgow, G4 0HZ, United Kingdom.

Conceived, designed and written by Julian Holland.

Maps by Lovell Johns Limited, Witney, Oxfordshire.
Edited by Colin Campbell and Tony Jervis.

A catalogue entry for this book is available from the British Library.

ISBN 978 1 84934 018 2
Printed and bound in the EU

CONTENTS

INTRODUCTION

Join Julian Holland on another nostalgic journey to discover Scotland's long lost railway heritage. Following on from his successful book, *Discovering Scotland's Lost Railways*, railway author and photographer Julian sets off again to discover the hidden secrets of more of those forgotten Scottish local railway lines. Despite some having a working life of fewer than 100 years, all of these lines were an important part of the communities that they once served and their loss is still felt across Scotland, from the far north and Deeside to the Borders and Galloway. Many of these lines had closed long before Dr Beeching came on the scene in 1963; their closures hastened by increasing competition from road transport in the 1930s and 1940s.

One such line was the Wick & Lybster Light Railway which closed in 1944. Few people know that the prohibition of alcohol sales in the town of Wick in 1922 gave this little line a new, albeit temporary, lease of life – from 28 May that year every pub and off-licence in the town was forbidden to sell alcohol but this did not stop some of the townsfolk in search of a bevvy travelling on the little railway to pubs and bars further down the line.

Royalty has also graced one of Scotland's long lost lines. Sadly missed today, the railway along Deeside from Aberdeen to Ballater changed the area dramatically, creating publicity through its use by royalty visiting Balmoral. Many important visitors to the castle, including the Tsar of Russia, travelled on the line – the last being Queen Elizabeth II who left on the last royal train from Ballater on 15 October 1965. Already listed for closure in the Beeching Report, the line closed for good a year later. Recently much of the old trackbed has been reborn as the Deeside Way footpath and cycleway, and has proved popular with commuters cycling to Aberdeen from its western suburbs.

From bridges, viaducts and cuttings to embankments, stations and tunnels, much of the infrastructure of Scotland's lost local lines still remains today. Easily traced on Ordnance Survey maps, these routes can be explored either on foot, bicycle or car. In these enlighted times many of them have been reopened as official footpaths and cycleways with car parks, picnic sites and even caravan parks often sprouting up at disused stations along the way.

Profusely illustrated with historical and present-day photographs, DISCOVERING SCOTLAND'S LOST LOCAL LINES brings to life the golden years of these railways and discovers what remains of them today. Go forth and enjoy!

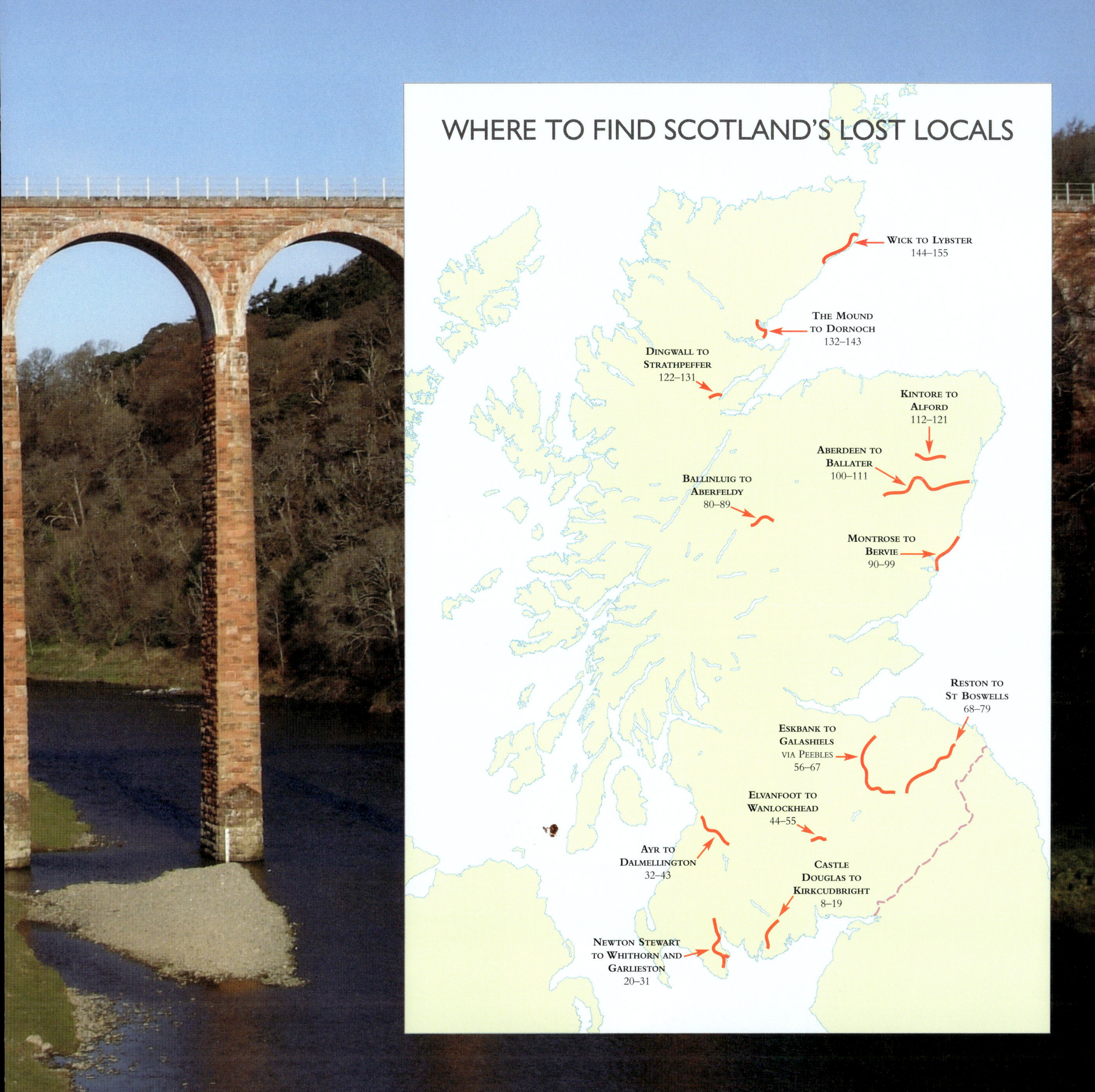
WHERE TO FIND SCOTLAND'S LOST LOCALS
Wick to Lybster
144–155
The Mound
to Dornoch
132–143
Dingwall to
Strathpeffer
122–131
Kintore to
Alford
112–121
Aberdeen to
Ballater
100–111
Ballinluig to
Aberfeldy
80–89
Montrose to
Bervie
90–99
Reston to
St Boswells
68–79
Eskbank to
Galashiels
via Peebles
56–67
Elvanfoot to
Wanlockhead
44–55
Ayr to
Dalmellington
32–43
Castle
Douglas to
Kirkcudbright
8–19
Newton Stewart
to Whithorn and
Garlieston
20–31

DUMFRIES, CASTLE DOUGLAS, and KIRKCUDBRIGHT.—Glasgow and South Western.

Miles	Down.	Week Days.											Suns.	
		mrn	mrn	mrn	mrn	mrn	mrn	aft	aft (Saturdays only.)	aft (Saturdays only.)	aft (Saturdays only.)	aft	mrn	
	812 Carlisle ....dep.	2 30	3 13	4 45	7 0	....	10 10	1 20	1 20	4 25	....	6 47	6 20	....
	Dumfries ....dep.	3 20	4 5	6 40	8 35	9 0	11 30	2 35	3 12	5 15	5 40	7 40	7 15	....
1¾	Maxwelltown	....	....	6 46	....	9 6	11 36	2 42	3 18	5 21	....	7 46	....	....
6	Lochanhead	....	....	6 55	....	9 15	11 45	2 52	3 27	5 30	....	7 55	....	....
8½	Killywhan	....	....	7 0	....	9 20	11 50	2 58	3 32	5 35	....	8 0	....	....
10½	Kirkgunzeon	....	....	7 6	....	9 26	11 56	3 4	3 38	5 41	....	8 6	....	....
12½	Southwick	....	....	7 12	....	9 32	12 2	3 10	3 44	5 47	....	8 11	....	....
14¼	Dalbeattie	....	4 31	7 18	9 5	9 39	12 8	3 18	3 51	5 52	6 7	8 17	7 47	....
19¾	Castle Douglas 872 ....arr.	3 53	4 40	7 28	9 15	9 50	12 18	3 28	4 0	6 2	6 17	8 27	8 0	....
73	872 Stranraer ....arr.	5A33	6A7	....	1120	....	....	5 38	....	....	8 15	....	....	....
—	Castle Douglas ....dep.	....	4 45	7 30	....	1010	12 20	3e40	4 2	6 5	....	8 30	....	....
22¼	Bridge of Dee	....	4 52	7 37	....	1017	12 27	3e47	4 9	6 12	....	8 39	....	....
26½	Tarff	....	5 2	7 47	....	1027	12 37	3e57	4 18	6 22	....	8 48	....	....
30	Kirkcudbright ....arr.	....	5 10	7 55	....	1035	12 45	4e5	4 25	6 30	....	8 55	....	....

Miles	Up.	Week Days.											Suns.	
		mrn	mrn	mrn	mrn	aft (Saturdays only.)	aft	aft	aft	aft	aft	aft	aft	
	Kirkcudbright ....dep.	6 30	8 50	....	11B0	1 0	1 5	2 45	4 45	....	7 15	....	....	....
3½	Tarff	6 39	8 59	....	11B9	1 9	1 14	2 54	4 57	....	7 27	....	....	....
7½	Bridge of Dee	6 49	9 9	....	11B19	1 19	1 24	3 4	5 7	....	7 37	....	....	....
10½	Castle Douglas 872 ....arr.	6 54	9 14	....	11B24	1 24	1 30	3 9	5 12	....	7 42	....	....	....
—	872 Stranraer ....dep.	....	....	7 35	9 30	....	....	....	....	3 40	....	9A55	....	....
—	Castle Douglas ....dep.	7 0	9 20	10 5	11 38	1 26	Except Saturdays.	3 20	5 14	5 57	7 44	11 30	9 0	....
15¾	Dalbeattie	7 12	9 30	10 18	11 52	1 36		3 30	5 24	6 8	7 54	....	9 20	....
17½	Southwick	7 17	9 36	....	....	1 41		3 36	5 29	....	7 59	....	....	....
19½	Kirkgunzeon	7 23	9 42	....	....	1 47		3 42	5 35	....	8 5	....	....	....
21¾	Killywhan	7 29	9 48	....	....	1 53		3 48	5 43	....	8 13	....	....	....
24	Lochanhead	7 35	9 54	....	....	1 59		3 54	5 49	....	8 19	....	....	....
28¼	Maxwelltown	7 44	10 4	....	....	2 8		4 4	5 58	....	8 28	....	....	....
30	Dumfries 813, 860 ....arr.	7 50	1010	10 43	12 15	2 15		4 11	6 5	6 37	8 35	12 1	9 55	....
63	813 Carlisle ....arr.	9 20	1130	12 5	2 37	3 30	....	6 5	8 17	8 17	9 55	12 47	12 0	....

NOTES.

A Stranraer Harbour.

B Mondays only.

e Except Saturdays.

CASTLE DOUGLAS TO KIRKCUDBRIGHT

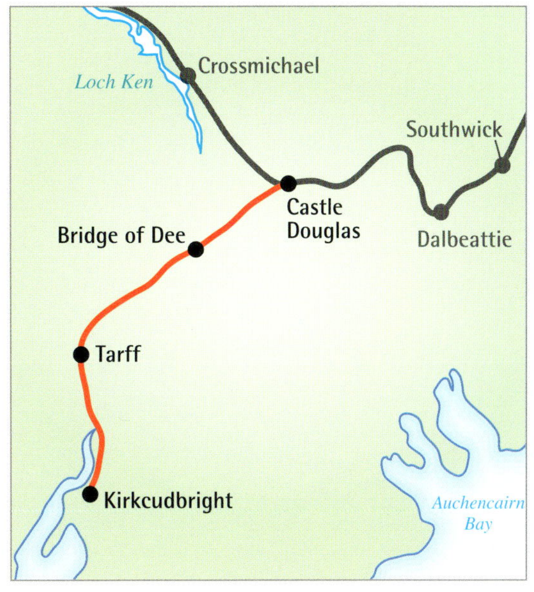

Named after the early Christian Saint Cuthbert, the county town of Kirkcudbright became a royal burgh in 1453. Located at the mouth of the River Dee, the town's harbour was once busy with the export of cloth from Scotland's mills while, today, its wide streets and attractive pastel-coloured houses are a reminder of the town's growth during the 19th century when the coming of the railway brought new prosperity. It was during this period that the town also became an artist's colony, attracting many artists, notably George Henry and E A Hornel, who travelled down from Glasgow by train. Hornel finally settled in the town in 1901 and his former home, Broughton House, is now owned by the National Trust for Scotland.

The first railway to reach this part of southwest Scotland was the Glasgow, Dumfries & Carlisle

Left *Trains for Castle Douglas would emerge from a cutting north of Kirkcudbright before approaching Tongland Viaduct on this low embankment. The centre spans of the viaduct were removed following closure of the line in 1965.*

Below *Ex-LMS three-cylinder compound 4P 4-4-0 No. 41132 halts at Castle Douglas with a Dumfries to Stranraer train on 1 June 1956. Built at Horwich Works in 1926, this locomotive was withdrawn from Stranraer engine shed (68C) only five months later.*

Left *'Black Five' 4-6-0 No. 44723 halts at Castle Douglas with a Stranraer Harbour to Dumfries train on 20 April 1965. Designed by William Stanier for the LMS, this locomotive was one of the last batch of its class to be built by British Railways at Crewe Works in 1949. It was finally withdrawn from Corkerhill shed (67A) on 31 October 1966.*

Railway which opened between Gretna Junction, north of Carlisle, and Dumfries in 1848. The following year the line was extended north to Closeburn and in 1850 met the rails of the Glasgow, Paisley, Kilmarnock & Ayr Railway between Cumnock and Auchinleck in Ayrshire. In that last year the two companies merged to become the Glasgow & South Western Railway.

The next railway to be built was the Castle Douglas & Dumfries Railway which opened between those two towns in 1859. Although nominally independent, the railway was worked from the outset by the Glasgow & South Western Railway and was later absorbed into that company in 1865. Castle Douglas was the end of the line until 1861 when the Portpatrick Railway opened across the wilds of Galloway to Stranraer and, the following year, to Portpatrick. This line connected with steamers for the short sea crossing to Northern Ireland and its story is told in *Discovering Scotland's Lost Railways.*

Despite all of this feverish railway activity the townsfolk and businessmen of Kirkcudbright were still more than 10 miles from their nearest station at Castle Douglas. They didn't have to wait long though, as the Kirkcudbright Railway, authorised in 1861, was opened from the town to Castle Douglas in 1864. Crossing the River Dee twice on stone viaducts at Tongland and Bridge of Dee, the single-track railway was absorbed into the Glasgow & South Western Railway a year later. Operating arrangements in the first few years were somewhat chaotic – although the line opened for goods on 17 February 1864 the Inspecting Officer refused to allow passenger trains to use Portpatrick Junction at Castle Douglas until new signalling had been installed and a speed restriction introduced. This remedial work was completed in August of that year but ongoing negotiations with the Castle Douglas & Dumfries Railway over joint use of its station led to a temporary station for Kirkcudbright trains being used at St Andrew Street until 1867.

For many years the town of Kirkcudbright and the intermediate stations at Tarff and Bridge of Dee had a fairly respectable passenger train service of seven return trains each weekday. As with all other Scottish branch lines there was no train service on the Sabbath. Sadly this frequency diminished in latter years due to ever-increasing competition from road transport and by 1964, a year before closure, this had dropped to three trains each weekday (plus one extra on Saturday) to Dumfries with four in the other direction. Bridge of Dee station had already closed on 26 September 1949 making Tarff the only intermediate station and passing loop on the line.

Along with numerous other Scottish branch lines, the railway to Kirkcudbright, together with the route from Dumfries to Challoch Junction (for Stranraer) was listed for closure in the 1963 Beeching Report. British Railways wasted no time in implementing the closure which came for the Kirkcudbright branch on 3 May 1965. The main line to Stranraer closed on 14 June 1965. The Kirkcudbright Railway had an operating life of just over 100 years and its disappearance is still felt by many local people today.

THE LINE TODAY

OS Landranger Map No. 84

Despite the passage of time since closure there is still much to see of the Kirkcudbright branch today. While the goods yard at Castle Douglas is now an industrial estate the goods shed still stands, albeit with a new lease of life as a timber warehouse. Immediately west of the town the line has disappeared following improvements to the A75 but from Kelton Mains, near Threave Castle, the trackbed as far as Bridge of Dee is now an official footpath. Bridge of Dee station is now a private residence while the goods yard and station house at Tarff is an agricultural supplier's depot. Despite the demolition of the central spans of Tongland Viaduct over the River Dee north of Kirkcudbright in 1966, two stone arches still stand on either bank of the river close to Telford's 1815 road bridge. Kirkcudbright station is now a beauty and fitness studio while the old toilet block is now the local bookie's office.

Above *West of Castle Douglas the trackbed of the branch line is now an official footpath linking Kelton Mains Open Farm and Bridge of Dee. Nearby is the National Trust for Scotland's Threave Castle and ornamental gardens.*

Right *Immaculately turned out by Carlisle Kingmoor shed (12A) ex-LMS 'Jubilee' Class 4-6-0 No. 45588 'Kashmir' waits at the head of the Stephenson Locomotive Society/Branch Line Society 'Scottish Rambler No 2 Joint Easter Rail Tour' on 15 April 1963. At the far end, BR Standard 2-6-4 tank No 80023 waits to take over the train down to Kirkcudbright. Built by the North British Locomotive Company in 1934 the 'Jubilee' was withdrawn in May 1965. With a working life of only 14 years, No. 80023 was withdrawn from Dumfries shed (68B) in November 1965.*

Left *Always keep a sharp look-out for clues to the past when walking along Scotland's old railway lines. Near Bridge of Dee, a mile or so west of Castle Douglas, this small, rusting bridge over Mill Burn can easily be overlooked by walkers on the railway path.*

Above *Frank Spaven's family have just joined the 2.50pm train from Dumfries, headed by a 'Black Five' 4-6-0, at Tarff station for a final hurl on the Kirkcudbright branch, just two weeks before its 3 May 1965 closure to passenger services.*

Above *A grimy ex-LMS Stanier Class 3 2-6-2 tank halts at litter-strewn Tarff station with a Dumfries to Kirkcudbright train on 30 July 1960. Based in the station yard since 1903, the Tarff Valley Agricultural Co-operative Society was supplied by rail with coal and lime until closure of the line in 1965.*

Below *These stone arches are all that is left of Tongland Viaduct over the River Dee north of Kirkcudbright. A similar pair can be seen in the grounds of a private residence on the north bank. Beyond is Telford's stone road bridge, built in 1815.*

Above *Hauled by BR Standard Class 4 2-6-4 tank No. 80074, a train from Dumfries and Castle Douglas rumbles across the Tongland Viaduct shortly before closure in May 1965.*

Above *British Railways lost no time in getting contractors to demolish the Tongland Viaduct following closure of the Kirkcudbright branch in 1965. Seen here in July 1966, Geo H. Campbell of Airdrie's crane lifts one of the steel girders away from the stone pillars that once supported the viaduct.*

Below *BR Standard Class 4 2-6-4 tank No. 80023 is the centre of attention at Kirkcudbright after working the SLS/BLS 'Scottish Rambler No 2 Joint Easter Rail Tour' down from Castle Douglas on 15 April 1963. The normally respectable railway enthusiasts often went to great lengths to obtain a photograph as witnessed here by the gentleman running across the track and one perched on top of the water tower.*

Above *Watched by a little boy and his mum, ex-LMS Stanier Class 3 2-6-2 tank No. 40170 heads out of Kirkcudbright with the 8.30am train to Castle Douglas on 4 June 1959. The photographer's car, a product of Reliant of Tamworth, waits patiently at the side of the road for its owner to return.*

Below *Seen here in the early 20th century, the overall roof at Kirkcudbright station was later replaced by a platform canopy. Opened in 1864 the station saw seven trains to Castle Douglas and Dumfries each weekday but by the 1960s, with increased competition from road transport, this had reduced to only three with one extra on a Saturday.*

Above *Overlooked by the tall spire of the town's parish church, ex-LMS Class 2P 4-4-0 No. 40577 waits to depart from Kirkcudbright with the 4.04pm to Dumfries on 16 April 1953. The photograph was taken by a young Richard Casserley whose famous father, Henry, can be seen taking a photo on the right. Built at Derby Works in 1928, No. 40577 was withdrawn from Dumfries shed (68B) in July 1961.*

Left *Kirkcudbright station building, seen here just before closure, was once the destination for artists from Glasgow, notably George Henry and E A Hornel, who were drawn to the town in the late 19th century.*

Right *Kirkcudbright station building is practically unchanged today. It is now enjoying life as a beauty and fitness studio while the former toilet block on the left (complete with satellite dish) is now the local bookie's shop. Modern housing now covers the former station site.*

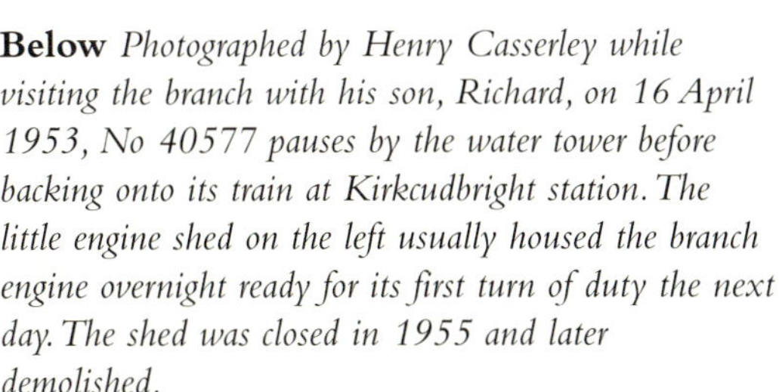

Below *Photographed by Henry Casserley while visiting the branch with his son, Richard, on 16 April 1953, No 40577 pauses by the water tower before backing onto its train at Kirkcudbright station. The little engine shed on the left usually housed the branch engine overnight ready for its first turn of duty the next day. The shed was closed in 1955 and later demolished.*

Mls								
	Whithorn ....dep.	7 35	9 20	....	1230	3 30	6 35	....
4	Millisie, for Garlieston ..	7 43	9 32	....	1238	3 39	6 42	....
5¾	Sorbie..............	7 48	9 41	....	1243	3 45	6 47	....
8¼	Whauphill	7 54	9 48	....	1248	3 52	6 52	....
10	Kirkinner	7 59	9 53	....	1252	3 57	6 56	....
12¼	Wigtown	8 5	10 3	....	1258	4 5	7 0	....
19¼	Newton-Stewart....arr.	8 20	1018	....	1 13	4 20	7 15	....

			aday morning	hts and Mond					nights and	hts and Mond		
—	Newton-Stewart ......dep.	....	6 45		....	....	....	8 35	1050	2 30	4 55	8 20
36¾	Wigtown	....	6 59		....	....	....	8 55	11 5	2 45	5 11	8 35
39	Kirkinner	....	7 3		....	....	....	9 5	1110	2 50	5 17	8 40
40¾	Whauphill	....	7 8		....	....	....	9 15	1116	2 56	5 23	8 47
43¼	Sorbie	....	7 3		....	....	....	9 25	1122	3 1	5 29	8 52
45	Millisle, for Garlieston ..	....	7 17		....	....	....	9 35	1127	3 6	5 37	8 57
49	Whithorn ....arr.	....	7 25		....	....	....	9 50	1137	3 14	5 45	9 5

NEWTON STEWART TO WHITHORN

The undulating Whithorn Peninisula has long been one of the most important farming areas in Scotland. Its fertile soils have for centuries supported dairy and arable farming, while the village of Garlieston with its natural harbour once supported a thriving fishing industry and was also the departure point for regular passenger sailings to Whitehaven, the Isle of Man and Liverpool.

By the mid-18th century nearly half of Wigtownshire was owned by one man, the 6th Earl of Galloway. In his time he was one of the first landowners in the country to introduce modern farming methods with larger farms and the planting of commercial forestry. Until the coming of the railway to Whithorn much of the agricultural produce and timber was shipped from the harbour at Garlieston.

Left *The substantial railway viaduct over the River Bladnoch south of Wigtown was the only major engineering feature on the meandering Wigtownshire Railway. The line was built to service the vast agricultural estates of the 10th Earl of Galloway.*

Below *With admiring glances from railway photographers, veteran ex-Caledonian Railway McIntosh Class 2F 0-6-0 No. 57375 trundles through Newton Stewart station on 15 April 1963 prior to working an enthusiasts special to Whithorn.*

Above *On 29 May 1965, with only two weeks to go before closure, a Stranraer to Dumfries train halts at Newton Stewart behind BR Standard Class 4 2-6-4 tank No. 80061. The freight-only branch to Whithorn had lost its passenger service in 1950 and closed completely on 5 October 1964.*

To the north the Portpatrick Railway had opened for business between Castle Douglas, Stranraer and Portpatrick in 1862. The nearest station on this line was then at Newton Stewart, some 19¼ miles north of the village of Whithorn. Eager to link his vast agricultural estates to the growing national rail system, the 10th Earl of Galloway played an important part in the building of the Wigtownshire Railway which was authorised by Parliament in 1872. With its headquarters at Wigtown, the railway opened in stages: Newton Stewart to Wigtown on 7 April 1875; Wigtown to Millisle on 2 August 1875; Millisle to Garlieston and Millisle to Whithorn on 9 July 1877. Apart from a bridge over the River Bladnoch south of Wigtown there were no major engineering features on this meandering line.

South from Newton Stewart there were stations at Wigtown, Kirkinner, Whauphill, Sorbie, Millisle (for the branch line to Garlieston) and Whithorn. In 1885 the Wigtownshire Railway amalgamated with its poverty stricken neighbour, the Portpatrick Railway, to form the Portpatrick & Wigtownshire Railway. The newly formed company was in fact jointly owned by four major railway companies, the Caledonian, Glasgow & South Western, London & North Western and Midland, all eager to keep the link to Stranraer and Northern Ireland open for their through traffic. However, this joint line was actually operated by the two Scottish companies.

Passenger traffic on the Whithorn branch line was never heavy and the service from Millisle to Garlieston ceased on 1 March 1903. The service to Whithorn consisted of four trains each weekday to Newton Stewart with an extra working on Fridays, presumably for the markets. In the opposite direction there were also four workings, one of them timed to connect with the sleeping car train from Euston, plus an extra Friday service.

Despite losing its passenger service in 1903 the Garlieston branch remained open for freight to and from the harbour until complete closure in 1964. This branch line was given a new lease of life in 1948 when a large rail-connected mill was built at the harbour to produce animal feeds for farmers in southwest Scotland. An early casualty of post-nationalisation rationalisation, passenger services between Newton Stewart and Whithorn ceased on 25 September 1950 but despite this, goods traffic, often in the charge of veteran Caley locomotives, continued to trundle up and down the line to Whithorn and Garlieston until complete closure on 5 October 1964.

THE LINE TODAY

OS Landranger Map No. 83

Today, much of the trackbed south of Newton Stewart as far as the outskirts of Wigtown is being slowly taken over by nature. Despite this, low embankments and a couple of road bridges still mark the course of the line.

At Wigtown a short section of the trackbed is now a footpath that closely hugs the salt marshes along the edge of Wigtown Sands to Wigtown Harbour. From here there are fine views across the bay to the Galloway Hills. South of Wigtown the substantial stone abutments of the viaduct across the River Bladnoch mark the only substantial engineering feature on this meandering rural line. Beyond here the overgrown route of the line through the villages of Kirkinner, Whauphill and Sorbie can often be spotted from the road – the former rail-connected creamery at Sorbie still stands with the building now being used by the Galloway Granite Company. At Millisle, former junction for the short branch to Garlieston Harbour, the station building is now a private residence. Nearly all traces of railway activity at Garlieston have recently disappeared beneath extensive residential development around the harbour.

Back at Millisle a footpath, reached by steps adjacent to bridge abutments, now runs southwards for a short distance along the railway embankment. The last three miles to Whithorn meander through the farming landscape, in places used as muddy farm tracks. The site of Whithorn station, a short distance to the north of the village close to the A746, is now a fire station.

Below *The tree line across the landscape at Barwhirran marks the route of the Wigtownshire Railway as it meanders through lush farmland south of Newton Stewart. Although nature is now taking over the trackbed, the small road bridge on the right is a continuing reminder of this long-closed railway.*

Below *At Wigtown the railway hugged close to the shore of Wigtown Bay. This stretch of the line is now a footpath to Wigtown Harbour and affords walkers fine views across Wigtown Sands to the Galloway Hills. Wigtown Sands is the largest Local Nature Reserve in Britain and supports a wide range of wildlife, particularly birds. The attractive small town of Wigtown is known as Scotland's National Book Town due to its wealth of second-hand book shops.*

Above *Seen here in happier days, the milk churns awaiting collection on the platform at Whauphill station are an indication of the railway's once important role for the dairy farmers of the Whithorn Peninsula.*

Above *Looking rather the worse for wear, ex-Caledonian Railway McIntosh Class 2F 0-6-0 No. 57375 passes through Whauphill station with a grain wagon and loaded timber wagons for Garlieston Harbour in 1963.*

Above *No. 57375 passes through closed Sorbie station en route for Garlieston Harbour with a load of grain and timber in April 1963. Reflecting the village's importance as the centre of a prosperous farming area, the building on the right is a creamery. On the left is a 'blood and custard' British Railways lorry. The creamery is long closed and the building is now the Galloway Granite Works.*

Left *A short stretch of trackbed along an embankment south of Millisle station is now a footpath. Millisle station, once the junction for the short line down to Garlieston Harbour, is a private residence.*

Below *The SLS/BLS 'Scottish Rambler No 2 Joint Easter Rail Tour' visited both the Kirkcudbright and Whithorn branches on 15 April 1963. Here the train has arrived at Garlieston, reached via a short branch line from Millisle Junction, behind branch engine No 57375. The tight curvature of the branch to Garlieston ruled out the use of bogie carriages so the enthusiasts, dressed in their best clothes, were instead carried in high-sided goods wagons.*

Above *Having just run an enthusiasts special down to Garlieston Harbour, regular branch engine No. 57375 arrives at Whithorn with a short freight train from Newton Stewart on 15 April 1963. Fitted with a stovepipe chimney, this vintage loco and the rusting rails it ran on were not long for this world – the line closed completely in October 1964. The station site at Whithorn is now a fire station. Introduced in 1883 a total of 244 of these Drummond-designed workhorses, known as 'Jumbos', were built for the Caledonian Railway with 239 surviving to BR days. By the time this photo was taken only 20 examples still survived.*

Left *At first glance this is just yet another muddy farm track but those with the 'knowledge' will know better! Here the Wigtownshire Railway once crossed a lane to Outon, one mile north of Whithorn.*

Below *When photographed on 23 June 1962 Whithorn station had been without a passenger service for 12 years. Goods trains continued to run down from Newton Stewart until complete closure of the line on 5 October 1964. The gentleman standing on the platform is railway photographer Henry Casserley.*

Above *The centre of much attention including a kilted photographer, branch engine No. 57375 runs round its train at Whithorn on 15 April 1963. The loco was hauling the SLS/BLS 'Scottish Rambler No 2 Joint Easter Rail Tour' between Newton Stewart, Garlieston and Whithorn. On the right is a classic '60s coach.*

Below *Preserved ex-GNoSR 4-4-0 No. 49 'Gordon Highlander' runs round its train at Whithorn on 23 June 1962. Together with preserved ex-CR 4-2-2 No. 123, the loco was hauling a joint SLS/RCTS week-long rail tour around the hidden byways of Scotland's rural railways.*

AYR, RANKINSTON, and DALMELLINGTON.—Glasgow and South Western.

Miles	Up.	Week Days only. mrn	mrn	mrn	mrn	aft	aft	aft	aft	aft	aft		
	Ayr ....dep.	....	9 30	....	11 40	....	2s30	4 10	6 45	8 30	9s30	....	....
6¼	Hollybush	....	9 47	....	11 57	....	2s47	4 27	7 6	8 47	9s47	....	....
11	Rankinston arr.	....	10 0	....	12 A 8	....	....	4 40	....	....	....	....	....
	Rankinston dep.	7 20	....	10A45	....	12 50	....	....	....	....	....	....	....
9¾	Patna............	8 g 1	9 58	11 A 5	12 8	1 10	2s57	4 38	7 17	8 57	9s57	....	....
11¾	Waterside	8 7	10 4	....	12 14	1 16	3 s 3	4 44	7 24	9 3	10 s 3	....	....
15	Dalmellington arr.	8 15	1010	....	12 20	1 24	3s10	4 50	7 32	9 10	10s10	....	....

Miles	Down.	Week Days only. mrn	mrn	mrn	mrn	aft	aft	aft	aft	aft	aft	
						Saturdays only.	Saturdays only.			Saturdays only.	Saturdays only.	
	Dalmellington dep.	7 15	9 15	10 35	....	12 45	3 40	4 5	....	6 0	7 40	....
3¼	Waterside	7 22	9 23	10 43	....	12 53	3 48	4 12	....	6 7	7 48	....
5¼	Patna............	7 27	9 28	10 48	11A35	12 58	3 54	4 18	....	6 13	7 54	....
10	Rankinston arr.	....	10 0	....	12 A 8	....	....	4 40	a	....	....	....
	Rankinston dep.	7 20	....	10A45	....	12 50	....	....	5 5	....	....	....
8¾	Hollybush	7 42	....	10 58	....	1 9	4 4	....	....	6 23	8 4	....
15	Ayr 819 to 823 arr.	7 53	....	11 10	....	1 22	4 18	....	5 50	6 37	8 17	....

A Tuesdays and Saturdays. a Through Train to Ayr, via Annbank, see page 822. g Arrives Patna at 7 45 mrn. s Saturdays only.

AYR TO DALMELLINGTON

With its numerous coal and ironstone mines and iron works, mineral-rich southern Ayrshire had become one of most important industrialised areas in Scotland by the mid-19th century. The rapid growth of industry in this region was entirely due to the building of the railways and the close proximity to harbours on the coast. The first railway in Scotland to be authorised by an Act of Parliament was the horse-drawn Kilmarnock & Troon Railway, which opened in 1812 to carry coal from pits at Kilmarnock down to the harbour at Troon. From 1817 the railway also became the first line in Scotland to use steam power.

Other mineral-carrying lines soon followed and in 1847 the Ayrshire & Galloway (Smithstown & Dalmellington) Railway was authorised to build a line up the Doon Valley to

Left *The major engineering feature on the Ayr & Dalmellington Railway, which opened in 1854, is the 17-arch Burnton Viaduct near Hollybush. Although passenger services on the line ended on 6 April 1964, the viaduct still sees the passage of coal trains from Minnivey open-cast mine.*

Below *Sporting its LMS number, ex-Caledonian Railway 'Dunalastair 1' Class 4-4-0 No. 14317 is seen here at Ayr's G&SWR station in 1930. Designed by John McIntosh and introduced in 1896, the Dunalastairs are rated as one of the most successful steam locomotive types built in Britain.*

A36

Waterside to serve the new Dalmellington Iron Company's coal and ironstone workings. The original aim of the railway's promotors was to extend the line southwards through the wilds of Galloway to meet the Portpatrick Railway at Castle Douglas, but by the time the first part of the railway had opened in 1854 it had changed its name to the Ayr & Dalmellington Railway and extended its route northwards to Falkland Junction at Ayr and southeasterly to terminate at Dalmellington. The line's major engineering feature is the 17-arch Burnton Viaduct near Hollybush. In 1858 the railway became part of the larger Glasgow & South Western Railway, and in 1872 a connecting line was opened from

Left *Ex-LMS 2-6-0 'Crab' No. 42861 storms uphill near Hollybush with the 10.15am train of empty coal wagons from Ayr Harbour to Waterside on 3 August 1965. Built at Crewe Works in 1930 this locomotive spent its last years working out of Ayr shed (67C), hauling coal trains on the Dalmellington branch until withdrawal in July 1966.*

Above *Near Holehouse Junction, the line to Rankinston is slowly being overtaken by nature. Despite this, modern signs at a nearby farm crossing warning of the passage of trains still remain today.*

Above *Overlooked by the signal box perched high above the cutting, the basic station at Holehouse was just an interchange platform for passengers using the branch line to Rankinston. The Rankinston branch lost its passenger services on 3 May 1950 but coal trains continued to use it for a few more years.*

Below *The twilight years of Scottish steam – 'Crab' 2-6-0 No. 42861 continues on its way up the Dalmellington branch as it approaches Holehouse Junction with a load of empty coal wagons from Ayr Harbour to Waterside on 3 August 1965.*

Holehouse Junction to Rankinston and Ochiltree on the Ayr to Cumnock line.

Despite being primarily a mineral-carrying line the Dalmellington branch had a fairly regular passenger service with five return journeys to and from Ayr each weekday with an extra two trains on Saturdays. At an exchange platform at Holehouse Junction, trains connected with the branch-line service to Rankinston which boasted three return services each weekday. Holehouse Junction is best remembered by railway photographers for its signal box which was built high above the snowdrift-prone cutting.

The Holehouse Junction to Rankinston and Ochiltree line closed to passengers on 3 May 1950 although coal trains still operated as far as Rankinston via Belston Junction to serve Littlemill Colliery for some time. Passenger services between Ayr and Dalmellington became an early casualty of the 'Beeching Axe' when they were withdrawn on 6 April 1964.

Freight traffic on the line was a completely different picture with trainloads of imported Spanish iron ore once struggling up the steep gradients from Ayr Harbour to the Dalmellington Iron Company's Works until the ironworks closed in 1921. Many of the collieries (now all gone) along the line were connected to the Dalmellington branch by private branch lines or inclines. The line was also a magnet for railway photographers in the years leading up to the end of steam in Scotland with Ayr engine shed's well-groomed 'Crab' 2-6-0s making a fine sight during their swansong as they struggled up the gradients with long trains of empty coal wagons. Despite closure to passengers and the end of steam, much of the Dalmellington branch is still open today serving an open-cast coal mine at Minnivey.

Below *In this wintry scene 'Crab' 2-6-0 No. 42800 storms through the cutting at Holehouse Junction with another load of empty coal wagons from Ayr Harbour on 2 March 1965. In the distance the lonely signal box is perched high above the often snow-filled cutting. The 'Crab' was withdrawn from Ayr shed eight months later.*

Above *Three female passengers make their way along the platform at Patna station after alighting from an Ayr to Dalmellington train on 3 July 1957. Along with the rest of the Dalmellington branch, Patna station lost its passenger service on 6 April 1964.*

Left *End of the line at Rankinston – 'Crab' 2-6-0 No. 42908 stands in the remains of Rankinston station before propelling a coal train to Belston Junction and from there onwards to Ayr. Judging by the burst of human activity some pretty vital track maintenance also seems to be under way on this little-used line.*

THE LINE TODAY

OS LANDRANGER MAP NO. 70

As the Ayr to Dalmellington branch is still open for coal traffic from Minnivey open-cast mine it would not be beyond the wit of man to reopen the line to passenger trains, a service that ended in 1964. Reinstatement of the last 1½ miles of line into Dalmellington would certainly be seen as a positive move for the residents of this neglected small town.

In the meantime Burnton Viaduct to the west of Hollybush is a notable landmark that still sees the passage of coal trains. The site of Holehouse Junction and the trackbed of the line to Rankinston can still be traced today although the famous signal box perched on the top of the cutting has long gone.

At Waterside, coal trains still rumble past the site of the station where the station house still stands, albeit in a poor state of repair. Close by, the former Dalmellington Ironworks (now known as Dunaskin Heritage Centre) is currently looking for a new owner. Meanwhile the Scottish Industrial Railway Centre, operated by the Ayrshire Railway Preservation Group, has built a small station here and laid a short section of track alongside the existing line to Minnivey. The centre owns a number of standard gauge steam and diesel industrial locomotives. For more details visit: www.arpg.org.uk

The final 1½ miles of trackbed to the western outskirts of Dalmellington is now a footpath.

Above *Although coal trains from Minnivey open-cast mine still rumble past the site of Waterside station, the station building – seen here from the rear – is now in a poor state of repair.*

Right *Formerly the Dalmellinton Ironworks, Dunaskin Heritage Centre near Waterside is currently looking for a new owner. Here the Scottish Industrial Railway Centre, operated by the Ayrshire Railway Preservation Group has built a small station and laid a short section of track alongside the existing line to Minnivey. The centre owns a number of standard gauge steam and diesel industrial locomotives.*

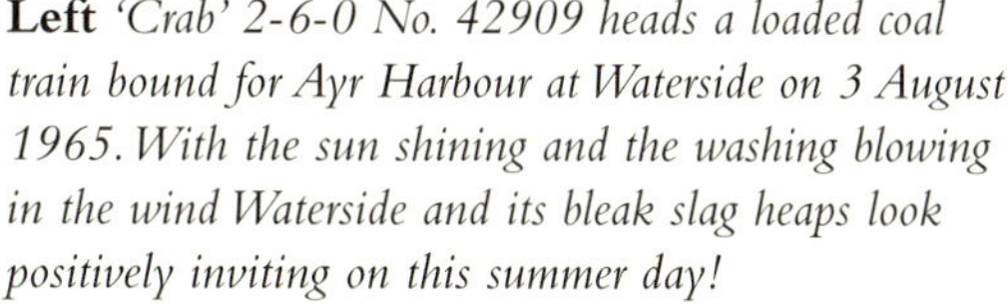

Left *'Crab' 2-6-0 No. 42909 heads a loaded coal train bound for Ayr Harbour at Waterside on 3 August 1965. With the sun shining and the washing blowing in the wind Waterside and its bleak slag heaps look positively inviting on this summer day!*

Above *With their smartly dressed stationmaster in the centre, the station staff at Dalmellington pose for the camera in LMS days. Scenes like this around Scotland were soon swept away after World War II with the nationalisation of Britain's railways and the wholesale closure of branch lines.*

Left *Railway photographer Henry Casserley visited the Dalmellington branch on 3 July 1957. His train from Ayr was hauled by ex-LMS Class 2P 4-4-0 No. 40640, here seen running round its carriages after arrival at the terminus, while the few passengers make their way towards the exit. No. 40640, built at Crewe in 1931, only had just over four years of active service left before withdrawal from Ayr shed in September 1961.*

Above *Due west of Dalmellington part of the line's old trackbed as far as the former junction with the line to Minnivey open-cast mine is now a footpath. The site of Dalmellington station has disappeared beneath an industrial estate. In an ideal world this short stretch of line could be reinstated to provide the folk of neglected Dalmellington with a train service to Ayr once again.*

ELVANFOOT, LEADHILLS, and WANLOCKHEAD.—Caledonian.

Miles.		Week Days only.						
				S	E	S		
		mrn	aft	aft	aft	aft		
—	**Elvanfoot** ....dep.	9 10	12 45	2 35	6 25	7 35	....	....
5¾	Leadhills...............	9 40	1 15	3 5	6 55	8 5	....	....
7¼	**Wanlockhead** ....arr.	9 50	1 25	3 15	7 5	8 15	....	....

Miles		Week Days only.							
				S	E	E	S		
		mrn	mrn	aft	aft	aft	aft		
—	**Wanlockhead** ......dep.	7 15	10 0	1 35	3 10	5 30	6 40	....	....
1½	Leadhills..................	7 25	10 10	1 45	3 20	5 40	6 50	....	....
7¼	**Elvanfoot 824, 831** arr.	7 50	10 35	2 15	3 50	6 5	7 20	....	....

E Except Saturdays. **S** Saturdays only.

ELVANFOOT TO WANLOCKHEAD

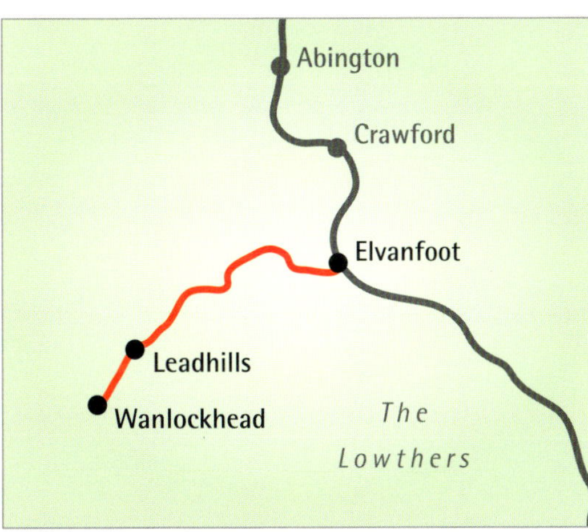

Left *The Wanlockhead branch clung to the north side of the Elvan Water valley as it made its way down towards Elvanfoot. Today, virtually all of the trackbed, seen here near North Shortcleugh, from Leadhills to Elvanfoot is accessible on foot or by mountain bike.*

For centuries, lead, gold and silver had been mined in the remote Lowther Hills in the Southern Uplands and then carried on the difficult overland journey to the port of Leith, near Edinburgh. Railways first reached this sparsely populated region of Scotland in 1848 with the opening of Elvanfoot station on the Caledonian Railway's main line between Carlisle and Glasgow. However, it wasn't until the end of the 19th century that serious thought was given to building a railway from Elvanfoot up to the mines in the Lowther Hills. Even in 1877 the Leadhills Silver-Lead Mining Company's request for a railway to serve its mines was turned down by the Caledonian Railway. Until 1896 the cost of building and operating such a line would have been prohibitive but in that year Parliament passed the Light Railways Act which allowed low-cost railways to be built in rural areas. Fencing, signalling, level crossings and station

Above *Carrying its LMS number, ex-Caledonian Railway Class 2P 0-4-4 tank No. 15181 waits to depart from Elvanfoot with the 12.19pm train for Wanlockhead on 30 July 1931. Built at St Rollox Works in 1907, this loco was withdrawn from Beattock shed (68D) in November 1951.*

platforms were no longer required but the act did limit weights to 12 tons per axle and imposed a speed restriction of 20mph and 8mph on bends. The fitting of cowcatchers on the locomotives was also mandatory on many of these lines. The scene was now set for 30 of these light railways to be built around Britain over the succeeding years.

One of the first of these railways to be built was the Leadhills & Wanlockhead Light Railway, which was promoted by the Caledonian Railway to connect the mines in the Lowther Hills with CR's main line at Elvanfoot. Engineered by Robert McAlpine ('Concrete Bob'), construction of the 7¼-mile line began in 1899 and involved the building of the eight-arch curving Rispin Cleuch Viaduct – a smaller version of Concrete Bob's famous Glenfinnan Viaduct on the Mallaig extension. Unlike Glenfinnan, Rispin Cleuch Viaduct was faced with terracotta bricks to hide its concrete construction. The line, worked from the outset by Caledonian, was opened to Leadhills on 1 October 1901 and to Wanlockhead a year later, and with a summit of 1,498ft above sea level was the highest standard gauge railway in Great Britain. During particularly hard winters the exposed line was often closed due to heavy snowfall.

Mines and smelters at Leadhills and Wanlockhead were connected to the new railway by narrow gauge feeder lines. The years following the opening of the railway were disappointing times for the local mining companies: the lead smelter at Wanlockhead closed in 1928. Closure of the mines came in 1931 but they were reopened for a short period in 1934 after which they closed for good.

Right *An early postcard view of Leadhills station taken just after opening of the line in 1901. On the right a goods train heads away from the station while in the centre lies, according to the postcard, Scotland's highest house. Although the line was closed in 1938, part of the trackbed between Leadhills and Wanlockhead was reopened in 1986 as a 2ft narrow gauge tourist line.*

Left *To the east of Leadhills the ballasted trackbed of the Wanlockhead branch provides a superb footpath through the remote Lowther Hills.*

Below *The major engineering feature on the line was the eight-arch curved Rispin Cleuch Viaduct. Built of concrete by 'Concrete Bob' McAlpine it was faced with terracotta bricks but was demolished in 1991 due to its poor state of repair. A mere roadside plaque now commemorates this act of vandalism!*

Below *The sweeping curve of the trackbed disappears westwards towards Leadhills around the lower slopes of Wellgrain Dod to the site of Rispin Cleuch Viaduct. The sites of old mines and spoil heaps that litter the landscape are a reminder of the once feverish mineral mining activity in this remote part of Scotland.*

Passenger services were also operated on the line by the Caledonian Railway and when the Garstang & Knott End Railway in Lancashire ceased running passenger trains in 1930, some of their coaches were moved to the Wanlockhead branch. Passenger services consisted of three trains each weekday to Wanlockhead, four in the opposite direction and two extra trains each way on Saturdays. With the closure of the mines the little railway's lifeblood drained away and it closed for good on 2 January 1939. Elvanfoot station on the Carlisle to Glasgow main line closed on 4 January 1965 and Rispin Cleuch Viaduct was demolished in 1991.

THE LINE TODAY

OS Landranger Map No. 78

Set in the remote and wild Lowther Hills, much of the former Wanlockhead branch line can easily be accessed on foot, by mountain bike or, at its western end, by narrow gauge railway.

Sadly, a viaduct over Elvan Water to the west of Elvanfoot has recently been demolished during the construction of a massive and ugly electricity substation. However, from the point where the line once crossed the B7040, the winding trackbed is easily followed on foot or by mountain bike as it climbs around the contours to Leadhills. While a detour is required at the site of Rispin Cleuch Viaduct the line can be followed to the current eastern extremity of operations of the narrow gauge Leadhills & Wanlockhead Railway.

From Leadhills to Glengonnar Halt, less than a mile short of the site of Wanlockhead terminus, this little line runs diesel-hauled passenger trains at Easter and at weekends from May until the end of September. Steam locomotives occasionally visit the line from other British narrow gauge lines. For more details visit the railway's website: www.leadhillsrailway.co.uk

Of particular interest at Leadhills station on Britain's highest adhesion railway is the signal box which was constructed using some of the terracotta facing bricks from the demolished Rispin Cleuch Viaduct. The mechanical

Above *The mines around Wanlockhead were once connected to the standard gauge line by 2ft gauge feeder railways. Here, Wanlockhead Mining Company 0-4-0 tank 'Wanlock', built by Andrew Barclay of Kilmarnock, and its crew poses for Henry Casserley's camera on 30 July 1931.*

Left *Ex-Caledonian Railway Class 2P 0-4-4 tank No. 15181 has just arrived at Wanlockhead with the 12.19pm train from Elvanfoot on 30 July 1931. Posing in front of the ex-Garstang & Knott End carriage is Kathleen Casserley who was accompanying her husband Henry on their honeymoon around Scotland's railways.*

equipment inside the box was originally in use on the West Highland Line.

When in operation the many mines and smelters around Leadhills and Wanlockhead were connected to the standard gauge line by narrow gauge feeder lines. The trackbeds of many of these tramways can still be followed on foot, in particular the track down from the Museum of Lead Mining at Wanlockhead past a restored beam engine to spoil heaps and derelict buildings of a mine in the Wanlock Water valley. This track is also used by walkers on the Southern Uplands Way Long Distance Path.

Above *A steam loco boiler and wagons await refurbishment at the eastern limit of current operations on the 2ft gauge Leadhills & Wanlockhead Railway. Opened in 1988 along part of the standard gauge trackbed of the Wanlockhead branch, this little railway currently operates diesel-hauled trains at Easter and on weekends between May and the end of September. An eastward extension of the line towards the B7040 is planned.*

Left *Although the site of the former terminus at Wanlockhead is now covered with sheep pens, the surrounding landscape is littered with old mines, winding gear, spoil heaps and the trackbeds of former narrow gauge feeder lines. The Museum of Lead Mining in the village – the highest in Scotland –features a tour of a lead mine and the second oldest subscription library in Europe.*

Above *Taken shortly after the opening of the line in 1902, the staff and train crew of a Caledonian Railway 0-4-4 tank pose for the camera at Wanlockhead station.*

Below *At 1,413ft above sea level, Wanlockhead was the highest standard gauge station in Britain.*

Above *Snow was a common factor to contend with during the winter on Britain's highest standard gauge line. Here the crew of Caledonian Railway 0-4-4 tank No. 1177 keep warm next to their gallant little steed at Wanlockhead in the early 20th century.*

Above *0-4-0 saddle tank No. 522 was used by Robert MacAlpine during the construction of the Leadhills & Wanlockhead Railway between 1899 and 1902. Seen here with with its crew and some construction workers, the loco was a product of Hudswell Clarke of Leeds.*

Right *Hauled by 0-4-0 diesel 'Clyde', a train on the Leadhills & Wanlockhead Railway approaches Leadhills station. The loco was built by Hunslet of Leeds in 1975 and first worked for the National Coal Board at Eppleton Colliery. Before arriving at Leadhills it was moved to the South Tynedale Railway at Alston.*

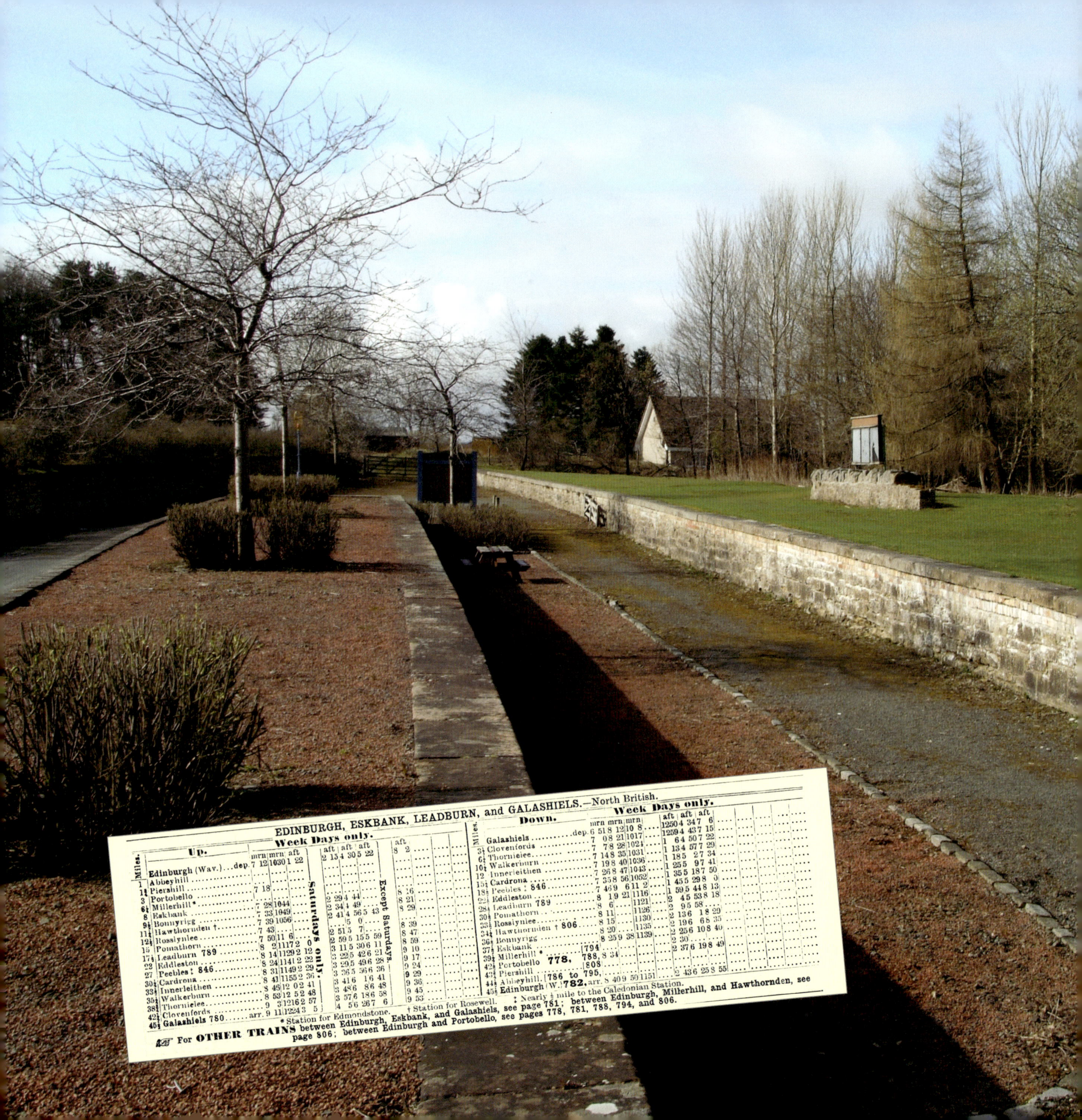

EDINBURGH, ESKBANK, LEADBURN, and GALASHIELS.—North British.

Miles.	Up.	Week Days only. mrn	mrn	aft (Saturdays only.)	aft	aft	aft (Except Saturdays.)	aft
	Edinburgh (Wav.) ... dep.	7 12	1030	1 22	2 15	4 30	5 22	8 2
1	Abbeyhill	....	....	....	....	....	....	....
1¾	Piershill	....	....	....	....	....	....	....
3	Portobello	7 18	....	....	....	....	....	....
6¼	Millerhill *	....	....	....	....	....	....	....
8	Eskbank	7 28	1044	....	2 29	4 44	....	8 16
9½	Bonnyrigg	7 33	1049	....	2 34	4 49	....	8 21
11¼	Hawthornden †	7 39	1056	....	2 41	4 56	5 43	8 29
12¾	Rosslynlee	7 43	....	....	....	5 0	....	....
15	Pomathorn	7 50	11 6	....	2 51	5 7	....	8 39
17⅓	Leadburn 789	8 2	1117	2 0	2 59	5 15	5 59	8 47
22	Eddleston	8 14	1129	2 12	3 11	5 30	6 11	8 59
27	Peebles ‡ 846	8 24	1141	2 22	3 22	5 42	6 21	9 10
30¼	Cardrona	8 31	1149	2 29	3 29	5 49	6 28	9 17
33½	Innerleithen	8 41	1155	2 36	3 36	5 56	6 36	9 24
35½	Walkerburn	8 45	12 0	2 41	3 41	6 1	6 41	9 29
38¾	Thornielee	8 53	12 5	2 48	3 48	6 8	6 48	9 36
42¼	Clovenfords	9 3	1216	2 57	3 57	6 18	6 58	9 45
45¾	Galashiels 780 ... arr.	9 11	1224	3 5	4 5	6 26	7 6	9 53

Miles.	Down.	Week Days only. mrn	mrn	mrn	aft	aft	aft
	Galashiels ... dep.	6 51	8 12	10 8	1250	4 34	7 6
3¼	Clovenfords	7 0	8 21	1017	1259	4 43	7 15
6¾	Thornielee	7 7	8 28	1024	1 6	4 50	7 22
10¼	Walkerburn	7 14	8 35	1031	1 13	4 57	7 29
12	Innerleithen	7 19	8 40	1036	1 18	5 2	7 34
15¼	Cardrona	7 26	8 47	1043	1 25	5 9	7 41
18¾	Peebles ‡ 846	7 35	8 56	1052	1 35	5 18	7 50
22¾	Eddleston	7 46	9 6	11 2	1 45	5 29	8 0
28¼	Leadburn 789	8 1	9 21	1116	1 59	5 44	8 13
30⅝	Pomathorn	8 6	....	1121	2 4	5 53	8 18
33⅛	Rosslynlee	8 11	....	1126	2 9	5 58	....
34½	Hawthornden † 806	8 15	....	1130	2 13	6 1	8 29
36⅛	Bonnyrigg	8 20	....	1135	2 19	6 6	8 35
37⅞	Eskbank	8 25	9 38	1139	2 25	6 10	8 40
39½	Millerhill *	....	....	....	2 30	....	....
42¾	Portobello	8 34	....	....	2 37	6 19	8 49
43¾	Piershill	....	....	....	....	....	....
44¾	Abbeyhill	....	....	....	....	....	....
45¾	Edinburgh (W.) 778, 782, 786 to 795, 788, 794, 808 ... arr.	8 40	9 50	1151	2 43	6 25	8 55

* Station for Edmondstone. † Station for Rosewell. ‡ Nearly ½ mile to the Caledonian Station.

☞ For **OTHER TRAINS** between Edinburgh, Eskbank, and Galashiels, see page 781; between Edinburgh, Millerhill, and Hawthornden, see page 806; between Edinburgh and Portobello, see pages 778, 781, 788, 794, and 806.

ESKBANK TO GALASHIELS VIA PEEBLES

Left *Now a picnic area, the well-tended platforms at Leadburn are located close to the crossroads of the A701 and the A6094. The station was once the junction for the North British Railway's branch line to Dolphinton, which closed in 1933. The line was later reopened from 1939 to 1960 to serve an army camp at Macbie Hill.*

Below *This large painted plaque in Peebles marks the site of the NBR station. The artist obviously didn't check his Ian Allan ABC book as the number is that of the Class J37 0-6-0 that hauled the last train.*

Set on the banks of the River Tweed, the small market town of Peebles was once an important centre for the woollen industry. Railways first came to the town as early as 1855 when the 19-mile Peebles Railway opened from Eskbank, south of Edinburgh. Although sponsored by the North British Railway, the Peebles concern operated the line with its own engines until 1861 when this was taken over by the NBR. The railway was finally absorbed by the NBR in 1876 by which time the town of Peebles, with its rail connections to Edinburgh, was becoming a popular health spa resort. In 1881 the Peebles Hydropathic Establishment was opened offering a wide range of mineralised water cures with clients being carried from the railway station by a horse-drawn bus. The Hydro was destroyed by fire in 1905 and the building we know today was opened in 1907.

Meanwhile, another railway had reached Peebles from the west. Originally seen by the Caledonian Railway as part of a grand cross-country route from Ayr to Berwick-upon-Tweed, the Symington, Biggar & Broughton Railway reached Peebles in 1864. The latter line involved the building of the graceful and still extant Neidpath Viaduct over the Tweed. The two separate stations in Peebles were linked by a bridge across the Tweed, although this was never used for regular passenger services. The railway map around Peebles was completed in 1866 when

Above *Following closure of the Hawthornden to Penicuik branch line to passengers on 10 September 1951, the nearest station to Penicuik was at Pomathorn on the Eskbank to Peebles line. Hence it was renamed 'Pomathorn for Penicuik'.*

Below *Leadburn station, seen here from an Edinburgh to Peebles train on 28 April 1952, featured one of the tall timber signal boxes found on this line. A new brick base was apparently being built at this time.*

the North British Railway opened an extension of the line from Eskbank eastwards along the Tweed Valley to Galashiels on the Edinburgh & Hawick Railway. The railway crossed and recrossed the River Tweed on graceful bowstring bridges that still survive today near Cardrona and Innerleithen.

Passenger train services between Edinburgh and Galashiels via Peebles (a circuitous route with a distance of 45½ miles) consisted of six return journeys each weekday. The Caledonian Railway's branch from Symington, on that company's main line between Carlisle and Glasgow, saw five return trips each weekday although passengers on the last train out of Peebles had to change at Biggar. For years the NBR and CR competed for customers visiting the Peebles Hydro by running expresses from Edinburgh – the Caley's was named the 'Tinto Express' although it took a longer route than the North British Railway's 'Peebles-shire Express'.

Surprisingly none of the railways to Peebles survived to see the Beeching Report of 1963. First to go was the ex-CR branch from Symington which closed to passengers on 5 June 1950. This was followed by the closure of the Eskbank to Galashiels via Peebles line on 5 February 1962, although at its northern end Bonnyrigg and Hawthornden stations (the latter by then called Rosewell & Hawthornden) remained open with a few trains to and from Edinburgh until 10 September 1962.

THE LINE TODAY

OS Landranger Maps Nos. 66 & 73

Despite closure nearly 50 years ago, much of the infrastructure of the Peebles Loop railway survives today. Apart from the stations at Peebles and Galashiels, all of the remaining 11 station buildings and/or platforms have survived in one form or another. Many are now private residences, with that at Innerleithen retaining its canopy and platform. Cardrona station with its attached small signal box has been beautifully restored and is now the local village store. At Leadburn the platforms and surrounding area have been landscaped as a picnic site.

There are also footpaths along the trackbed at several locations, notably at Hawthornden, Peebles (where a new cyclepath has been opened through the short tunnel under Innerleithen Road), Cardrona (where the bridge over the Tweed leads to the local golf course) and at Innerleithen (where a footpath crosses the Tweed on a recently restored bridge). At the end of the line, Galashiels patiently awaits the planned reopening of the Waverley Route northwards to Edinburgh in 2014.

Right *Before passing through the grounds of Peebles Hydro the line to Galashiels once passed under this stone bridge that now forms the entrance to a small housing development in the town.*

Above *Milk churns and station staff stand on the platform of Eddleston station in the early 20th century. The single-storey station building is now a private residence.*

Below *This elegant cast-iron footbridge once crossed a railway cutting in the grounds of Peebles Hydro. The cutting has since been filled in.*

Right *Two immaculately dressed trainspotters (aka the photographer's sons, David and Malcolm Spaven) leave the 8.59am arrival from Edinburgh at Peebles's single-platform station on the last day of service, Saturday 3 February 1962. The photographer, Frank Spaven, was the first head of planning at the Highlands & Islands Development Board and is credited with saving the Highland lines to Thurso, Wick and Kyle of Lochalsh from closure.*

14/5/58
GALASHIELS
VIA PEEBLES
B

Above *Horse-drawn buses wait outside Peebles's North British Railways station waiting to take customers to the Peebles Hydropathic Establishment which had opened in 1881.*

Above *The busy single-line platform at Peebles East sees the arrival of a North British Railways train from Edinburgh in the early 20th century. At this time the station was the destination of the 'Peebles-shire Express' which carried customers for the Peebles Hydro from Edinburgh.*

Right *Between Peebles and Galashiels the railway crossed and recrossed the River Tweed at four locations. Here, at Cardrona, this fine bowstring set of bridges now carries a track to the local golf club.*

Above *Cardrona station was the first station out from Peebles on the extension to Galashiels opened by the North British Railway in 1866. The station building and signal box survive today as a village store. North of the station the five-span bowstring bridge over the River Tweed is now part of the Cardona Golf Club.*

Right *This restored six-span bowstring bridge now carries a footpath over the River Tweed on the eastern outskirts of Innerleithen.*

Below *The signal box, station building and platform at Cardrona are now home to the village store.*

Left *Innerleithen signal box, seen here on 28 April 1952, was a lofty wooden affair perched on a brick base similar to that at Leadburn further up the line. The station building here is now a private residence while the six-span bowstring bridge over the Tweed has been recently restored as part of a footpath and cycleway.*

Left *Walkerburn station was once served by around six trains each day between Peebles and Galashiels. The station building, stationmaster's house and goods shed still survive today albeit with different uses. The author remembers staying in a spooky hotel, reminiscent of the location of an Agatha Christie whodunit, in the former woollen mill village in 1971.*

Below *Viewed from a Galashiels-bound train, Clovenfords station looked spick and span on 28 April 1952. As with the photo of Walkerburn above, there is no evidence of any customers: hardly surprising in this sparsely populated rural area.*

Above *Galashiels, also the junction for the Selkirk branch and the Waverley Route, was a fairly busy place until the closure of the Peebles Loop. Here, in June 1958, a Peebles train has arrived at the station behind ex-NBR Class D30/2 4-4-0 No. 62437 'Adam Woodcock' of St Margaret's shed, while another loco waits to haul the empty stock away. The D30/2 had only another month in service before withdrawal.*

Right *The Waverley Route was a popular destination for enthusiasts specials during the final years of steam in Scotland. Here, ex-LNER Class A4 4-6-2 No. 60031 'Golden Plover' of St Rollox shed (65B) pauses at Galashiels in April 1965 before resuming its journey. This iconic locomotive was withdrawn only six months later. The Waverley Route closed on 6 January 1969 but the planned reopening between Edinburgh and Tweedbank in 2014 will see trains returning to Galashiels once again.*

ST. BOSWELLS, DUNS, RESTON, and BERWICK.—North British.

Miles	Down.		Week Days only. mrn	mrn	mrn	aft	aft
	St. Boswells	dep.	6 23	8 33	1110	4 5	6 15
4½	Earlston		....	8 42	1120	4 15	6 27
10½	Gordon		....	8 54	1132	4 27	6 41
14½	Greenlaw		....	9 3	1141	4 39	6 55
18¼	Marchmont		....	9 10	1149	4 47	7 5
22	Duns	arr.	7 2	9 17	1157	4 55	7 15
		dep.	7 12	10 0	1240	5 1	7 25
25¼	Edrom		7 20	10 8	1248	5 9	7 33
26¾	Chirnside		7 24	1012	1252	5 13	7 37
30¾	Reston * 776	arr.	7 33	1021	1 [illegible]	5 22	7 46
		dep.	7 36	1024	1 6	5 26	....
34¾	Ayton		7 43	1032	1 14	5 33	....
36½	Burnmouth		7 49	1038	1 20	5 39	....
42	Berwick	arr.	7 57	1046	1 28	5 48	....

Miles	Up.		Week Days only. mrn	mrn	aft	aft	aft	aft
	Berwick	dep.	....	8 30	1250	3 28	....	....
5½	Burnmouth		....	8 41	1 2	3 39	....	....
7¼	Ayton		....	8 46	1 7	3 44	....	....
11¼	Reston	arr.	....	8 54	1 14	3 52	....	....
		dep.	....	8 58	1 18	3 56	6 40	8 2
15¼	Chirnside		....	9 8	1 28	4 6	6 50	8 12
16¾	Edrom		....	9 12	1 32	4 10	6 54	8 17
20	Duns	arr.	....	9 20	1 40	4 18	7 2	8 25
		dep.	7 10	9 29	1 43	4 21	....	....
23¾	Marchmont		7 18	9 37	1 51	4 29	....	....
27½	Greenlaw		7 27	9 46	2 0	4 38	....	....
31½	Gordon		7 36	9 55	2 9	4 47	....	....
37½	Earlston [and below		7 49	10 8	2 22	5 0	....	....
42	St. Boswells 780, 781	arr.	7 59	1018	2 32	5 10	....	....

* Station for Coldingham (3¼ miles) and St. Abbs (4¼ miles).

For **LOCAL TRAINS** between Reston and Berwick, see page 776.

RESTON TO ST BOSWELLS

Opened in 1846, the North British Railway's line from Edinburgh to Berwick-upon-Tweed was an important link in the East Coast Main Line that we know today. The North British also lost no time in building branch lines from the main line and, in 1849, the company opened an 8¾-mile double-track line from Reston, on the mainline, inland to Duns. The hoped-for traffic from this sparsely populated agricultural region never materialised and the line was singled in 1857. However, this lack of success didn't stop the promoters of the Berwickshire Railway building a 22-mile extension from Duns to St Boswells. The extension was authorised in 1862 and opened throughout in 1865. The major engineering feature on this rural line was the magnificent 19-arch Leaderfoot Viaduct just north of St Boswells. The viaduct still stands today and is now a Grade A listed structure.

The Berwickshire Railway amalgamated with the North British Railway in 1876 and settled down to a fairly quiet existence punctuated by extremely busy moments when cattle were sent to market in St Boswells from stations along the line. Following these markets a steady stream of cattle trains would then steam south to England via the Waverley Route. Passenger traffic was fairly light with only four through trains from St Boswells to Berwick via Reston running each weekday plus an extra train terminating at Reston. In the opposite direction there were only

Right *A thoughtful touch – the North British Railway fitted these attractive drinking taps, such as this one at Reston, for thirsty travellers on all of its station platforms.*

Left *A landmark to drivers on the A68 north of St Boswells, the 19-arch Leaderfoot Viaduct over the River Tweed last saw the passage of a train in July 1965. The viaduct is now a Grade A listed structure.*

Above *Ex-LNER Class J39/3 0-6-0 No. 64844 of Tweedmouth shed (52D) trundles through Reston en route for the Duns branch in September 1960.*

Above *The first station out from Reston on the Berwickshire Railway was at Chirnside, seen here in the 1950s – the small child standing by the signal box appears to be enjoying a sandwich. The platform and station building survive today.*

three through trains each weekday plus a couple of isolated services between Reston and Duns.

No doubt this remote rural railway would have been closed by the early 1950s but an act of God brought about an even earlier demise. Heavy rainfall and flooding in early August 1948 swept away part of the railway between Greenlaw and Duns. Passenger services between St Boswells and Duns ceased immediately, never to return. The section of line between Reston and Duns reverted to its original branch-line status but that, too, lost its passenger service on 10 September 1951. Freight trains from St Boswells continued to cross Leaderfoot Viaduct to Greenlaw until 19 July 1965; freight services between Reston and Duns ceased on 7 November 1966. The Berwickshire Railway, never delivering the traffic forecast by its over-optimistic Victorian promoters, was finally dead.

THE LINE TODAY

OS LANDRANGER MAPS NOS. 67 & 74

Although Reston station on the East Coast Main Line between Berwick and Edinburgh closed to passengers on 4 May 1964, local pressure groups are hoping that it may be reopened in the near future. Until then, this part of Berwickshire will have been devoid of any railway service for nearly 50 years.

Thankfully, for lovers of Scotland's lost railways, much of the infrastructure of the Reston to St Boswells line is still intact. To the south of Reston, the stations and platforms at Chirnside and Edrom survive along with the goods shed at the latter station. Despite recent development at Duns, part of the station building is now a private residence while a builder's merchant now makes use of the former goods yard. The next station along the line was at Marchmont, built to serve nearby Marchmont House – today the restored station with its well-tended platform makes a fine sight nestling in the picturesque valley of Howe Burn. Further west, the station buildings at both Greenlaw and Gordon are now private residences while the road overbridges at both these sites still remain in situ. One mile to the west of Gordon, Gordon Moss, where train drivers once stopped to dig peat for the station garden at St Boswells, is now a wildlife reserve.

The *pièce de resistance* of the Berwickshire Railway must surely be the graceful 19-arch Leaderfoot Viaduct across the River Tweed two miles north of St Boswells. Restored by Historic Scotland in the 1990s, the viaduct is now a Grade A listed structure and is best viewed from the old Drygrange road bridge (built in 1780 and now closed to traffic) and away from the busy A68. Although currently closed to pedestrians there is a possibility that the viaduct may be reopened to walkers in the future. The station at St Bowells has been demolished although rail services are due to reopen as far as Galashiels and Tweedbank when the northern half of the Waverley Route is reopened in 2014.

Above and below *The Reston to Duns section of the Berwickshire Railway was built as a double-track line. However, the expected traffic never materialised and it was soon singled. Even today, all of the bridges on this section, such as this one to the east of Duns, clearly show their extravagant width.*

Above and left *Superpower derailment at Duns! Standing in for the usual Standard Class 3 2-6-0 from Tweedmouth shed (closed because it was an English Bank Holiday), 'Peak' Class diesel D181 became derailed at Duns while hauling the branch freight on 30 August 1965. Heavy lifting gear hauled by D5180, seen here on the left, arrived from Gateshead and eventually got the 'Peak' back on track.*

Right *The section of the Berwickshire Railway between Greenlaw and Duns was closed completely in 1948 following severe flooding. Here the trackbed can be seen winding its way up the valley of the Howe Burn near Marchmont station. Built to serve nearby Marchmont House, the station has been restored as a private residence.*

Above *Headed by ex-NBR Class D34 4-4-0 No. 62471 'Glen Falloch', the Branch Line Society's 'Scott Country Rail Tour' visited Greenlaw on 4 April 1959. The locomotive was withdrawn less than a year later although a sister engine 'Glen Douglas' has since been preserved and from May 2011 will be displayed at the new Riverside Museum in Glasgow.*

Left *Following the floods of 1948 Greenlaw became the eastern terminus of the Berwickshire Railway from St Boswells. Here, on 15 May 1958, ex-NBR Class J35 0-6-0 No. 64494 shunts the branch freight train after arriving from St Boswells.*

Right *Although the station at Greenlaw is now a private residence, the bridge that once carried the A6105 over the railway still stands. To the east of the bridge the trackbed curves away to cross Blackadder Water on its route to Marchmont and Duns.*

Above *The answer lies in the soil – headed by ex-NBR Class J35 0-6-0 No. 64494, the Greenlaw to St Boswells freight train pauses at Greenlaw Moss on 15 May 1958 while the crew fill bags of peat destined for the station garden at St Boswells.*

Left *The Berwickshire Railway approached Gordon station from the west through a long, sweeping cutting. Today the road bridge still stands, the station building is now a private residence and the trackbed has been recently resurfaced.*

Above *The station staff at Gordon pose for the camera in the early 20th century. The station closed to passengers in 1948 after severe flooding damaged the line between Greenlaw and Duns. Goods services continued until 16 July 1965. Both the station building and platform survive today.*

Above *A scene never to be repeated as the last freight train from St Boswells to Greenlaw pauses at Gordon on 16 July 1965 while the crew pose for the camera.*

Above *Seen here in 1963, Earlston station had two platforms, a passing loop, sidings, goods shed and cattle dock. The latter would have been busy during market days when cattle were sent by train to St Boswells.*

Right *Another scene of the last freight train to Greenlaw on 16 July 1965. This time it is at Earlston while the crew and a local family pose beside diesel shunter D3888. On good authority the author has been told that the gentleman in the cab was based at Hawick MPD while the two other men are Norman Jeffrey (holding the youngster) and Bill Butler. The photographer's own abiding memory of that last day was watching the train returning to St Boswells with the young lad, held by his Mum, on the back of the guard's van waving the guard's green flag for all he was worth!*

Right *Final day of service – hauled by diesel shunter D3888, the last freight train from Greenlaw slowly crosses the graceful Leaderfoot Viaduct on 16 July 1965.*

Left *Opened in 1865 to carry the Berwickshire Railway over the River Tweed north of St Boswells, Leaderfoot Viaduct is now a Grade A listed structure. Keen eyes will notice that the central stone pier is not perfectly vertical.*

Below *BR Standard Class 2 2-6-0 No. 78047 stands at St Boswells with a single coach train for Kelso in March 1963. Passenger services along the Tweed Valley between St Boswells and Tweedmouth ceased on 13 June 1964. The single-track line saved British Railway's bacon in 1948 when the East Coast Main Line between Grantshouse and Reston was washed away in floods – main line expresses such as the non-stop 'Flying Scotsman' were rerouted along the line to St Boswells where they continued on up the Waverley Route to Edinburgh. The same happened in 1954 when the 'Elizabethan' express was diverted via Kelso.*

ABERFELDY and BALLINLUIG.—Highland.

Miles	Week Days only.		mrn	mrn	aft	aft	aft	aft	
	Aberfeldy	dep.	7 0	9 25	12 20	1 20	5 0	8 0	....
4¼	Grandtully		7 10	9 35	12 30	1 30	5 10	8 10	....
8¾	Ballinluig 868	arr	7 20	9 45	12 40	1 40	5 20	8 20	....

Miles	Week Daysonly.		mrn	mrn	aft	aft	aft	aft	
	Ballinluig	dep.	7 40	10 30	1250	2 5	5 30	8 30	...
4¼	Grandtully		7 50	10 40	1259	2 20	5 40	8 40	...
8¾	Aberfeldy	arr.	8 0	10 50	1 8	2 30	5 50	8 50	...

BALLINLUIG TO ABERFELDY

Railways first came to this part of the Highlands in 1856 with the opening of the Perth & Dunkeld Railway. The line north from here to Inverness via Ballinluig, Pitlochry and Aviemore was built by the Inverness & Perth Junction Railway, which opened in 1863 – two years later the two companies amalgamated to form the Highland Railway. The coming of the railway brought Victorian visitors in their thousands, eager to see the beauty of the Highland scenery, and led to the development of the towns and villages along its route.

Nine miles to the east of Ballinluig lay the busy, historic town of Aberfeldy, until the coming of the railway an important crossing point on the River Tay. The importance of a rail connection was vital for the town's cotton mills and distilleries, and a provision for an 8¾-mile branch

Left *This bridge once carried the Aberfeldy branch over the River Tay one mile west of Ballinluig. Although privately owned, the bridge is now open for the passage of light vehicles, cyclists and pedestrians. Route 7 of the National Cycle Network also takes in the bridge on its 214-mile route from Glasgow to Inverness.*

Below *A southbound freight headed by Highland Railway 'Jones Goods' 4-6-0 No. 103 pulls out of Ballinluig's freight yard for Perth, c.1920. This loco has been preserved and from May 2011 can be seen at the new Riverside Museum in Glasgow. Ballinluig, along with the Aberfeldy branch, closed on 3 May 1965.*

Above *In the final years before closure the one-coach Aberfeldy passenger trains were hauled by powerful Type 2 diesels. Here, a Birmingham Railway Carriage & Wagon Company loco (Class 26) has arrived at Ballinluig with a train from Aberfeldy on 9 March 1963. The branch goods train is on the left.*

Right *Another view of the old railway bridge across the River Tay at Logierait, one mile west of Ballinluig. With 41 bridges along its 8¾-mile route the Aberfeldy branch proved to be a costly project for the Highland Railway. The line closed in 1965, just two months short of its centenary.*

line from Ballinluig had been included in the 1861 Act authorising the building of the main line northwards from Dunkeld.

Winding its way along the south bank of the River Tay, the single-track Aberfeldy branch, with an intermediate station at Grandtully, opened on 3 July 1865. With its 41 bridges, including two major structures over the Rivers Tummel and Tay to the west of Ballinluig, the line was not cheap to build. Now easily reached by train from the south, Aberfeldy, with its hotels and easy access to fishing on the Tay, soon became a popular destination for Victorian travellers.

Train services on the line were fairly modest and timed to connect with trains on the Highland Railway's main line at Ballinluig. Right up until closure there were six trains each way on weekdays but none on the Sabbath. An extra intermediate stop was included in 1935 when a halt was opened at Balnaguard. Along with many Scottish branch lines the Aberfeldy branch was listed for closure in the 'Beeching Report' of 1963; despite this the little line hung on for two more years, by then its single coach train was being hauled by a modern Type 2 diesel. Freight services were the first to go on 25 January 1965 with passenger services ending on 3 May that year – just two months before its 100th birthday!

THE LINE TODAY

OS LANDRANGER MAP NO. 52

Although the site of Ballinluig station has disappeared beneath improvements to the A9 trunk road and the bridge over the River Tummel has been replaced by a modern road bridge, the lasting memorial to the Victorian builders of the Aberfeldy branch is the elegant steel bridge over the River Tay just one mile to the west. The bridge is privately owned but open for the passage of light vehicles, cyclists (on Route 7 of the National Cycle Network) and pedestrians.

To the west of the bridge, the route of the line can be followed alongside the B898 past the site of Balnaguard Halt to the outskirts of Grandtully. Here the station site, complete with platform and road overbridge, has been incorporated as part of a new caravan site.

Between Grandtully and Aberfeldy the old railway runs beside the winding A827 as it threads its way along the valley of the River Tay. In parts the trackbed is a footpath while it is also used as a farm track and as access to private residences.

At Aberfeldy the station site has disappeared but on the eastern outskirt of the town the once rail-connected Aberfeldy Distillery features a preserved Andrew Barclay 0-4-0 tank locomotive, once the distillery's 'Puggie', displayed on a short length of track.

Below *Old style Aberfeldy motive power – more suitably adapted for branch-line work, ex-Caledonian Railway 0-4-4 tank No. 55212 stands at Ballinluig station with the 10.28am train to Aberfeldy on 12 July 1957. Built at St Rollox Works in 1911, this loco was withdrawn from Perth shed at the end of 1958.*

WARNING
PRIVATE BRIDGE
ALL USERS DO SO AT THEIR OWN RISK
PAINTED
47 30
4
EPAINTED 2000-2001

Above *The 10.28am train to Aberfeldy leaves Ballinluig behind No. 55212 on 12 July 1957 and approaches the castellated bridge over the River Tummel. One of the two major engineering features on the line, the bridge has since been replaced by a new road bridge.*

Left *Beyond the bridge over the River Tay the trackbed of the Aberfeldy branch reverts to a farm track. A mile further on lies the site of Balnaguard Halt.*

Right *Balnaguard Halt, seen here in July 1957, was opened in 1935. Basic facilities, amounting to an oil lamp, small wooden shelter and sleeper-built platform were provided for passengers.*

Above and below *A popular destination for anglers on the River Tay, Grandtully was the only intermediate station on the Aberfeldy branch. The station is seen in the early 20th century (above) and on 12 July 1957 (below) when the parcels traffic, then an important revenue earner for BR, still seemed to be thriving.*

Left and above *The station site at Grandtully has recently been reopened as a caravan site. Although the station building has been demolished the old goods platform and road overbridge still lend a distinctive railway atmosphere to the place.*

Left *An animated scene at Aberfeldy on 22 August 1961 with the arrival of the branch train from Ballinluig behind ex-CR 0-4-4 tank No. 55217. The parcels traffic still seems to be holding up well while a young trainspotter has a serious discussion with the driver.*

Below *The 10.28am train from Ballinluig has just arrived at Aberfeldy on 12 July 1957. Mixed trains were the order of the day on many Scottish branch lines – here the two-coach train ran with the goods wagons attached at the rear.*

This page *Although Aberfeldy station no longer exists there is still much to see in the grounds of the once rail-connected Aberfeldy Distillery. Here, the distillery's former 0-4-0 'Puggie' tank locomotive, built by Andrew Barclay of Kilmarnock in 1939, and a wagon loaded with wooden casks have been restored on a short length of track.*

MONTROSE and BERVIE.—North British.

Miles frm Montrose	Down.	Week Days only. mrn	mrn	aft	Saturdays only. aft
	782 Edinburgh (Wav.) dep.	4 12	7 40	2 20	4 25
	782 Dundee (Tay Bridge) "	5 38	9 33	3 51	6 32
	782 Arbroath "	6 4	10 8	4 25	7 9
—	Montrose dep.	7 5	10 54	5 10	7 38
3¼	North Water Bridge	7 14	11 3	5 19	7 47
5½	St. Cyrus	7 20	11 9	5 25	7 53
6¼	Lauriston	7 24	11 13	5 29	7 57
8½	Johnshaven	7 30	11 19	5 35	8 3
10	Birnie Road Siding	....	....	f	....
12	Gourdon	7 38	11 27	5 43	8 11
13	Bervie arr.	7 42	11 31	5 47	8 15

f Stop on Fridays only.

Miles	Up.	Week Days only. mrn	aft	aft	Saturdays only. aft
	Bervie dep.	7 48	12 57	5 53	8 20
1	Gourdon	7 52	1 0	6 1	8 24
3	Birnie Road Siding	f	....	....	....
4½	Johnshaven	8 1	1 10	6 16	8 33
6¾	Lauriston	8 8	1 16	6 22	8 39
7¾	St. Cyrus	8 12	1 20	6 26	8 43
9¾	North Water Bridge	8 18	1 26	6 32	8 49
13	Montrose § 784 arr.	8 27	1 35	6 41	8 58
26¾	784 Arbroath arr.	9 1	2 24	7 15	....
43¾	784 Dundee (Tay Bridge) "	9 44	2 47	7 38	....
103	784 Edinburgh (Wav.) "	11 55	4 38	9 20	....

§ Over ½ mile to Caledonian Station.

MONTROSE TO BERVIE

By the 19th century the east coast harbour town of Montrose had become an important centre for the fishing industry, a major importer of Scandinavian timber and a major exporter of Scottish wool. To serve this growing trade the first railway to be built to the town arrived in 1848. The branch line extended from Dubton Junction on Aberdeen Railway's line from Guthrie to Aberdeen. The company amalgamated with the Scottish Midland Junction Railway in 1855 to become the Scottish North Eastern Railway which itself was then absorbed by the Caledonian Railway in 1866.

The next railway to arrive at Montrose was the 13-mile Montrose & Bervie Railway which was operated from its opening in 1865 by the Caledonian Railway. The line had originally been been backed by the Great North of Scotland

Left *Hugging the North Sea coastline the Bervie branch line approached the fishing village of Gourdon behind a low sea wall. Its route through the village is now marked by a line of modern houses that have been built on the trackbed. To the north of the village the trackbed is now a coast-hugging cycleway and footpath.*

Below *The former Caledonian Railway terminus in Montrose, seen here after closure in 1934, was originally opened by the Aberdeen Railway in 1848 and later used by the Montrose & Bervie Railway until 1881 when the North British Railway opened its own through station in the town.*

Above *North of Montrose the Bervie branch crossed the River North Esk on the 11-arch North Water Bridge. Part funded by local philanthropist Alexander Christie, the adjacent single-track road bridge was completed in 1776.*

Railway which saw it as forming part of a greater Aberdeen Junction Railway but this was never built. The Montrose & Bervie was later absorbed by the North British Railway in 1881 with trains for the branch using that company's station in Montrose via a short spur from Broomfield Junction. The major engineering feature on the line was the 11-arch North Water Bridge Viaduct which still stands today.

A third railway, the North British, Arbroath & Montrose Railway, reached Montrose in 1881, by which time that company had been amalgamated with the North British Railway. Montrose was now served by two separate stations, half a mile apart: (a) the NBR station on the line that was eventually to become part of the East Coast Main Line that still operates today; and (b) the Caledonian Railway's terminus. The latter station, served by trains from Brechin and Bridge of Dun via Dubton Junction was closed in 1934.

Built to serve fishing villages along the coast north of Montrose, the Bervie branch settled down to a meagre three return trains each weekday plus an extra evening service on Saturdays. Following nationalisation of Britain's railways in 1948 the newly formed British Transport Commission's Branch Line Committee lost no time in closing many loss-making Scottish branch lines. Included in this list of closures was the Bervie branch which lost its passenger service on 1 October 1951. As with many of these lines, goods trains continued to run for some years but the end finally came for the Bervie branch, steam-hauled to the end, on 23 May 1966 when it was closed completely.

THE LINE TODAY

OS LANDRANGER MAPS NOS. 45 & 54

The former North British Railway station at Montrose is still served by trains on the East Coast Main Line while the former Caledonian Railway terminus in the town has been converted into a nursing home. North of Montrose the sturdy North Water Bridge over the River North Esk still stands as the major engineering feature on the Bervie branch. Although none of the station buildings along the line have survived, much of this coastal route can be traced to the east of the A92. Punctuated at intervals by solitary road overbridges and occasional embankments, the trackbed often disappears completely beneath ploughed fields as if it had never existed.

At the northern end of the branch line the former trackbed can be followed along the sea wall on the southern approach to Gourdon while modern housing has been built along the route of the line through the village. To the north it is now a well-surfaced footpath and cycleway that acts as a traffic-free deviation for National Cycle Network Route 1 as far as Bervie.

Right *Ex-NBR Class J37 0-6-0 No. 64608 passes through Lauriston with the daily freight train from Bervie to Montrose on 5 August 1965. Steam-hauled to the end, the Bervie branch finally closed just over nine months later.*

64608

Above *Seen alongside the A92 road the route of the Bervie branch between St Cyrus and Johnshaven often completely disappears beneath ploughed fields. Here, a blocked up road bridge marks the southern limit of a caravan and camp site on the site of Lauriston station.*

Left *The joint SLS/RCTS 1960 Scottish Railtour again – this time seen pausing at Johnshaven on 16 June with Bert Hurst posing for Henry Casserley's camera.*

Right *The end is nigh as No. 64608, star of the Bervie daily freight on 5 August 1965, passes through overgrown Johnshaven with the return freight to Montrose. Judging by the light load this was definitely a loss-making venture by then but it is still a sight for sore eyes today. Pure nostalgia!*

Above *Viewed from a road bridge, the trackbed of the Bervie branch at Johnshaven is now a landscaped footpath. The station site in the village has disappeared beneath new housing.*

Above *Ex-NBR Class J37 0-6-0 No. 64608 meanders along the coastline near the harbour village of Gordoun with the daily freight to Montrose just before closure of the line in May 1966. Introduced in 1914, many of these sturdy locos survived until the end of steam in Scotland.*

Above *Headed by ex-NBR Class J37 No. 64615 the SLS/RCTS 1960 enthusiasts special pauses at Gordoun on 16 June. The stack of wooden packing cases on the platform are a reminder of the once important local fishing industry and its dependence on the railway to transport fresh catches to market.*

Right *The Bervie branch approached the fishing village of Gourdon from the south behind this sea wall. The conveyance of fresh fish from the villages along the line to distant markets was once an important source of revenue for the railway.*

64608
VGE 460

Above *North of Gourdon the coastal route of the railway to Bervie is now a well-surfaced footpath and cycleway that acts as a traffic-free deviation for National Cycle Network Route 1. The rusting remains of cast iron fence posts mark the course of the line along this scenic route.*

Left *The end of the line at Bervie on 5 August 1965 – ex-NBR Class J37 0-6-0 No. 64608 simmers gently alongside the platform that last saw passenger trains in 1951. The British Railways lorry and the two young onlookers add a touch of 1960s nostalgia to this evocative picture.*

Above *The branch passenger train from Montrose is pictured here after arriving at Bervie in the early 20th century. Along with many other Scottish branch lines, the Bervie branch lost its passenger service during the drastic cost-cutting period following nationalisation of Britain's railways in 1948.*

ABERDEEN TO BALLATER

Left *The Deeside Way footpath and cycleway, seen here alongside restored Cambus O'May station, now uses the trackbed of the Ballater branch for much of its route from Aberdeen Duthie Park.*

Below *Until Aberdeen Joint Station was opened in 1867, trains from Banchory on the Deeside Railway terminated at Guild Street station. The joint station, seen here with its John Menzies outlet c.1960, was rebuilt in the First World War and has recently been redeveloped yet again.*

Railways first came to Aberdeen with the opening of the Aberdeen Railway from Guthrie to Ferryhill in 1850. From the north, the Great North of Scotland Railway had opened the first part of its line from Kittybrewster to Huntly in 1854. However, the railway up Royal Deeside from Aberdeen to Ballater was built in fits and starts. The first proposal for a line to Banchory was made as early as 1845 but it wasn't until 1853 that the Deeside Railway opened for business between the newly opened

Above *Following nationalisation in 1948, ex-Great Eastern Railway Class B12 4-6-0s were drafted to Aberdeen Kittybrewster shed. Here No. 61552 drifts past Ferryhill shed as it approaches Aberdeen with the 3.30pm from Ballater on 16 June 1949.*

Below *An early view of Drum station on the Deeside line. An extension of the Deeside Railway from Drum to Alford had been proposed in 1856 but this lost out in favour of the rival Alford Valley Railway which was built from Kintore (see pages 112–121).*

Guild Street station in Aberdeen and Banchory – until the building of Aberdeen Joint Station in 1867 lines from the south had terminated at Guild Street while those from the north terminated at Waterloo station. The 16½-mile line along Deeside eventually included 12 intermediate stations plus a private station for Crathes Castle.

The opening of the railway to Banchory soon led to proposals for a westward extension to Aboyne. Known as the Deeside Extension Railway, this nominally independent 15¼-mile line was promoted by and worked from the outset by the Deeside Railway. Opened from a new station at Banchory in 1859, the extension featured four intermediate stations including one at Lumphanan which was reached via a two-mile deviation northwards away from the Dee Valley. A fifth station, Dee Street Halt was not opened until 1961, just four years before closure.

Effectively one through railway between Aberdeen and Aboyne, the two railways were leased by the Great North of Scotland Railway in 1866. With the new physical connection via the new joint station in Aberdeen that opened the following year the GNoSR had now reached the southernmost limit of its railway empire. The Deeside Railway and the Deeside Extension Railway were eventually absorbed by the GNoSR in 1875.

The final chapter of the railway up Royal Deeside also came in 1866 when the Aboyne & Braemar Railway – sponsored by the Deeside Railway and the GNoSR – was opened for 11 miles as far as Ballater. The line to Braemar was never built, probably at the request of Queen Victoria, but an extension to Bridge of Gairn, designed to serve the forestry industry west of Ballater, was started yet never completed although its earthworks can still be seen today. The GNoSR was one of the first railways in the UK to introduce motorbuses to connect with their rail services and from 1904 visitors to Braemar were carried a further 16 miles up the valley from Ballater station.

To the east, the section of the original Deeside Railway between Ferryhill and Culter was relaid as double track in 1893 allowing a frequent suburban service to operate serving eight intermediate stations. By 1922 these trains had become so popular that there were 18 return trips each day with Culter also being served by the other trains on the Banchory and Ballater run. Four of these trains terminated at Banchory while another five continued on to Ballater. Journey time for the 43¼-mile journey was around 1hr 40min although one fast up train in the morning and down in the late afternoon took about 1hr 10min. The suburban services ceased after World War II and the line from Aberdeen Ferryhill to

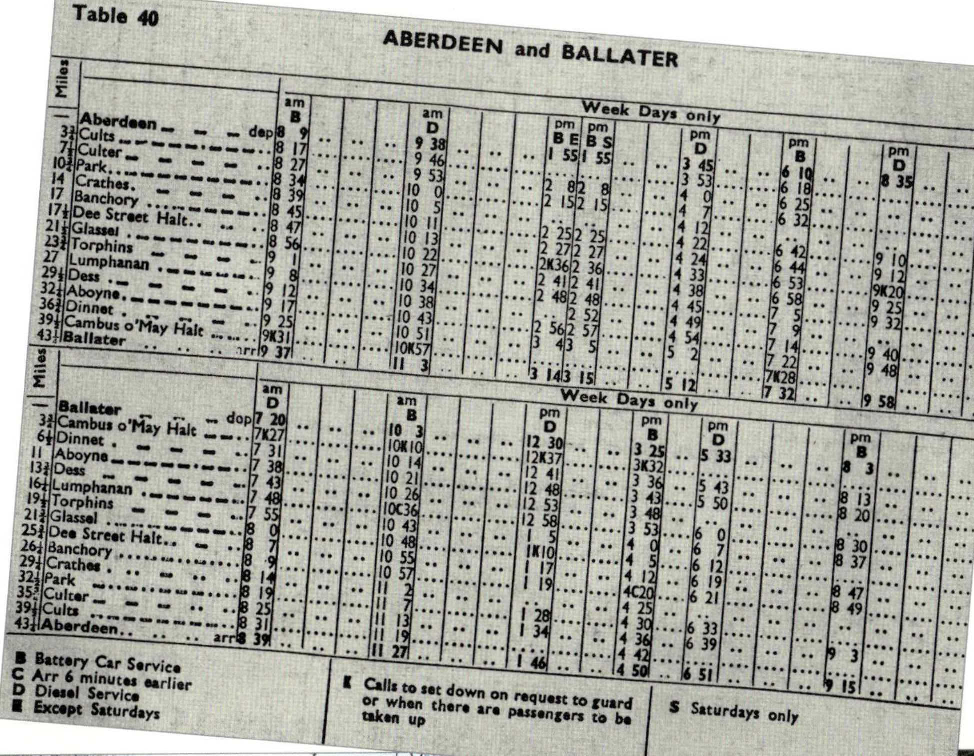

Table 40

ABERDEEN and BALLATER

Week Days only

Miles		am B	am D	pm B E	pm B S	pm D	pm B	pm D
—	**Aberdeen** dep	8 9	9 38	1 55	1 55	3 45	6 10	8 35
3¾	Cults	8 17	9 46	..	..	3 53	6 18	..
7½	Culter	8 27	9 53	2 8	2 8	4 0	6 25	..
10¾	Park	8 34	10 0	2 15	2 15	4 7	6 32	..
14	Crathes	8 39	10 5	..	..	4 12	..	..
17	Banchory	8 45	10 11	2 25	2 25	4 22	6 42	9 10
17½	Dee Street Halt	8 47	10 13	2 27	2 27	4 24	6 44	9 12
21½	Glassel	8 56	10 22	2K36	2 36	4 33	6 53	9K20
23¾	Torphins	9 1	10 27	2 41	2 41	4 38	6 58	9 25
27	Lumphanan	9 8	10 34	2 48	2 48	4 45	7 5	9 32
29½	Dess	9 12	10 38	..	2 52	4 49	7 9	..
32¼	Aboyne	9 17	10 43	2 56	2 57	4 54	7 14	9 40
36¾	Dinnet	9 25	10 51	3 4	3 5	5 2	7 22	9 48
39½	Cambus o'May Halt	9K31	10K57	..	..	..	7K28	..
43¼	**Ballater** arr	9 37	11 3	3 14	3 15	5 12	7 32	9 58

Week Days only

Miles		am D	am B	pm D	pm B	pm D	pm B
—	**Ballater** dep	7 20	10 3	12 30	3 25	5 33	8 3
3¾	Cambus o'May Halt	7K27	10K10	12K37	3K32	..	..
6½	Dinnet	7 31	10 14	12 41	3 36	5 43	8 13
11	Aboyne	7 38	10 21	12 48	3 43	5 50	8 20
13¾	Dess	7 43	10 26	12 53	3 48	..	..
16¼	Lumphanan	7 48	10C36	12 58	3 53	6 0	8 30
19½	Torphins	7 55	10 43	1 5	4 0	6 7	8 37
21¾	Glassel	8 0	10 48	1K10	4 5	6 12	..
25¾	Dee Street Halt	8 7	10 55	1 17	4 12	6 19	8 47
26¼	Banchory	8 9	10 57	1 19	4C20	6 21	8 49
29¼	Crathes	8 14	11 2	..	4 25	..	..
32½	Park	8 19	11 7	1 28	4 30	6 33	..
35¾	Culter	8 25	11 13	1 34	4 36	6 39	9 3
39½	Cults	8 31	11 19	..	4 42	..	..
43¼	**Aberdeen** arr	8 39	11 27	1 46	4 50	6 51	9 15

B Battery Car Service
C Arr 6 minutes earlier
D Diesel Service
E Except Saturdays

K Calls to set down on request to guard or when there are passengers to be taken up

S Saturdays only

Below *Today, the Deeside Way footpath and cycleway passes through Culter station en route to Ballater. The station was once served by an intensive suburban passenger service stopping at all stations to Aberdeen.*

Left *Apart from some gaps and deviations the Deeside Way footpath and cycleway makes use of most of the Deeside line's trackbed between Aberdeen Duthie Park and Ballater. Here, it is seen passing through farmland alongside the A93 between the sites of Park station and Crathes station.*

Above *This Edwardian view of Banchory station features several of the new fangled automobiles that were eventually to become the downfall of the Deeside line. Banchory was the western terminus of the line from Aberdeen until the opening of the Deeside Extension Railway to Aboyne in 1859.*

Park was singled. By then competition from road transport had brought a decline in both goods and passenger services to the line.

During the British Railways era, in an effort to reduce running costs, the Deeside line service to Ballater saw the introduction of a unique two-coach battery-electric railcar in April 1958 – this was recharged overnight either at Ballater or Aberdeen. Despite some technical problems the multiple unit remained in service until closure of the line and was affectionately known as 'The Sputnik'. The remaining steam services were phased out in July 1958 and replaced by diesel multiple units. Listed for closure in the previous year's Beeching Report, by 1964 the writing was on the wall for the Deeside line. Train services to Ballater had been reduced to six each way a day with three of these being operated by the battery unit. Despite much local outcry the end came on 28 February 1966 when passenger services ceased. Goods services between Culter and Ballater ended on 18 July while the section from Ferryhill to Culter closed on 2 January 1967. Barely 100 years old, the Deeside line was dead.

The Balmoral estate further up the Dee Valley to the west of Ballater had been purchased in 1848 for Queen Victoria as a retreat and the Deeside line will always be remembered for its royal trains bringing the Royal Family and dignitaries to Balmoral Castle. The first recorded use of the railway by a reigning monarch was in 1853 when Victoria and Albert took a train from Banchory, then the end of the line, for the journey back down south to London. Carrying the Prince and Princess of Wales, the first royal trains to use Ballater were in September 1866, before the station had even been opened to the public. Royal trains continued to travel up to Ballater until the year before closure – on 15 October 1965 Queen Elizabeth made her last journey from the station. Another feature of the Deeside line were the Royal Messenger Trains that ran every day when the Royal Family were in residence in Balmoral. Connecting with the overnight train from London these unadvertised trains began in 1865 and continued until 1938.

THE LINE TODAY

OS LANDRANGER MAPS NOS. 37 & 38

A large proportion of the trackbed of the closed Ballater branch has recently been reopened by Aberdeenshire Council and other organisations including Sustrans as a traffic-free footpath and cycleway known as the Deeside Way. Currently the route starts in Duthie Park in Aberdeen, close to the former site of Ferryhill engine shed and, apart from a short diversion around Drumoak, faithfully follows the old railway as far as Banchory. Although the long section from here to Aboyne has yet to be completed, the Deeside Way recommences at Aboyne and continues past Dinnet and Cambus O'May stations to end at the beautifully restored Ballater station.

There is much to interest lovers of old railways along the route, including the restored platforms at Culter where there is a small car park, the Royal Deeside Railway at Milton of Crathes, the base of the water tower and the engine shed at Banchory (a garden machinery shop), the former station building at Aboyne (now used to house shops) and the restored stations at Cambus O'May and Ballater.

The Royal Deeside Railway has laid track for over a mile from their headquarters at Milton of Crathes towards Banchory and runs trains on most weekends between April and September. The unique two-car battery DMU that once operated on the Ballater branch is preserved here. For more details visit: www.deeside-railway.co.uk

Right *The recently opened Deeside Way again, this time west of Aboyne passing through dense coniferous woodland adjacent to Dinnet station where the station building (now an estate office), platform and level-crossing gateposts remain intact.*

Above *Aboyne became the western terminus of the Deeside line from Aberdeen from 1859 to 1866 when the Aboyne & Braemar Railway opened as far as Ballater. Although closed in 1966 the station fortunately survived and is now home to a range of shops. Between closure and restoration the canopied station platform, pictured above c.1970, appears to have been put to good use by young local footballers.*

Above *Restored Cambus O'May station overlooks the Deeside Way footpath and cycleway.*

Above *Not a customer in sight. Only a solitary set of footprints offer any clue to life at snowbound Cambus O'May station in December 1962.*

Right *The unusual name of Cambus O'May comes from the Gaelic, meaning 'river bend in the plain'. It was also the name of the penultimate station on the Deeside line, seen here from a Ballater-bound train on 9 July 1957. A graceful suspension footbridge, still in use today, connected the station to the south bank of the River Dee.*

GENTLEMEN
CAMBUS O MAY

Above *In an effort to reduce running costs steam-hauled trains on the Deeside line were eliminated in 1958 to make way for a unique battery-powered railcar and diesel railcars. However, steam still reigned supreme when this photograph was taken of Ballater station on 9 July 1957. On the left BR Standard Class 4 2-6-4 tank No. 80028 waits to depart with the 3.30pm to Aberdeen while on the right No. 80113 is setting back onto its train.*

Left *The unique BR-built battery railcar made up of units SC79998 and SC79999 leaves Banchory for Aberdeen on its first day of public service, 21 April 1958. Locals nicknamed it 'The Sputnik'! The remaining steam services on the Deeside line were replaced by diesel multiple units in July of that year. Despite this cost-cutting exercise passengers voted with their cars and the Deeside line was doomed.*

Right *A deserted Ballater station on 2 June 1965 with a two-car DMU patiently waiting for some customers for Aberdeen. By this date the Deeside line was living on borrowed time and closure was fewer than nine months away. Despite much local outcry, the closure had become inevitable since Dr Beeching's Report in 1963. The rusting rails and empty platforms tell the same sad story that had already been repeated throughout the UK – the car and lorry had won and, without strong local patronage, lines such as these were doomed. This lesson surely should be remembered for Scotland's few remaining rural lines – use it or lose it.*

Below *Superbly restored, Ballater station now houses a Tourist Informaton Centre, café and an exhibition on royalty. Beyond the station a road bridge marks the start of the uncompleted extension to Braemar. It is thought that its construction was halted by Queen Victoria who objected to mass public transport passing through her beloved Balmoral estate.*

KINTORE and ALFORD.—Great North of Scotland.

Miles.	Down.	Week Days only. mrn	mrn	aft	aft	
	Kintore ....dep.	7 57	1034	4 23	6 32	....
4½	Kemnay	8 9	1043	4 35	6 41	....
7¾	Monymusk	8 15	1049	4 41	6 47	....
10¾	Tillyfourie	8 22	1057	4 49	6 55	....
13	Whitehouse	8 28	11 4	4 56	7 2	....
16	Alford ....arr.	8 33	1110	5 2	7 8	....

Miles.	Up.	Week Days only. mrn	mrn	aft	aft	
	Alford ....dep.	7 0	8 50	1 45	5 35	....
3	Whitehouse	7 6	8 56	1 51	5 41	....
5¼	Tillyfourie	7 12	9 2	1 57	5 47	....
8¼	Monymusk	7 19	9 9	2 4	5 54	....
11½	Kemnay	7 27	9 17	2 12	6 2	....
16	Kintore 865 and [above arr.	7 36	9 25	2 20	6 13	....

KINTORE TO ALFORD

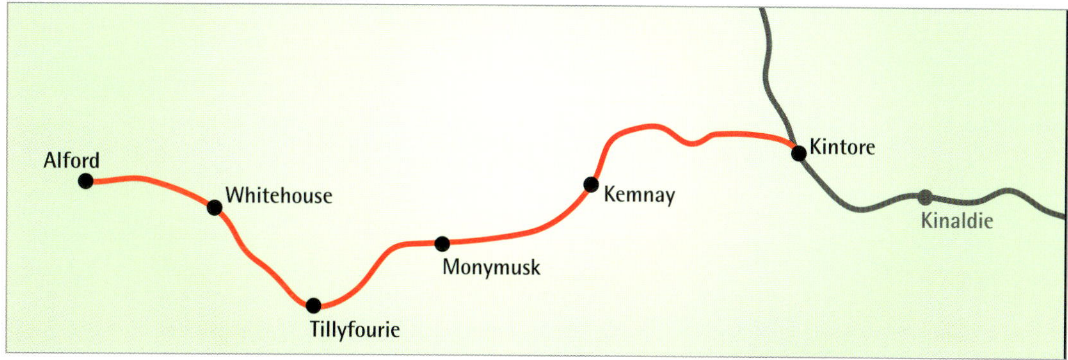

Left *West of Kemnay the route of the Alford branch through Aberdeenshire farmland is easily spotted alongside the B993. All traces of the railway in the village have disappeared beneath housing development.*

Below *Kintore station on the Great North of Scotland Railway's main line from Aberdeen to Keith was also the junction for the Alford branch. Here, in the early 20th century, a train is seen approaching from the south while the branch bay platform on the right looks decidedly deserted. Reopening of Kintore station is a possibility in the future.*

The first part of the Great North of Scotland Railway's main line from Aberdeen to Keith opened as far as Huntly in 1854. The line had been a long time in gestation; its construction was delayed because of a widespread financial crisis in 1847. The opening of this line spawned many other schemes for feeder branch lines designed to tap into the important agricultural region of Aberdeenshire, enabling farmers to transport cattle and crops long distances to more lucrative markets.

One such scheme was the Alford Valley Railway which despite a lot of false starts was authorised in 1856 to build a 16-mile branch

Nº 49

from Kintore, on the GNoSR main line, to Alford thus thwarting a rival scheme to reach this large but remote village from the Deeside Railway at Drum. Promoted by the GNoSR, which also offered to work it, the steeply graded line was opened on 21 March 1859. Intermediate stations were at Kemnay, Monymusk and Whitehouse while an additional station at Tillyfourie was opened the following year.

Passenger traffic on the line was never heavy and the four return trains each weekday sufficed requirements. The train engine was kept overnight in a small engine shed at Alford in readiness for working the first train of the day, usually around 7am, to Kintore where there was a bay platform for the branch-line trains. Here trains connected with services between Aberdeen and Keith. However, freight traffic on the line was much more important with agricultural produce and cattle being transported to markets some distance away. A sawmill at Monymusk and granite quarries at Tillyfourie and Kemnay also produced much traffic for the line.

Despite this, traffic receipts were disappointing and the nominally independent Alford Valley Railway was soon in financial difficulties. It was saved from bankruptcy in 1862 by the GNoSR which took over the line completely four years later. The branch trains continued to trundle up and down the line until after World War II when the newly formed British Transport Commission produced a long list of loss-making Scottish branch lines that they wanted to close – the Alford branch was on this list and passenger trains

Left *Despite closure to passengers in 1950 the Alford branch occasionally saw the passage of an enthusiasts special. Here, preserved ex-GNoSR Class D40 4-4-0 No. 49 'Gordon Highlander' halts at Monymusk on 13 June 1960. The throng of well-dressed and well-behaved railway enthusiasts might well have been fascinated by the old coach body sitting on the opposite platform – it is a 28ft third-class coach built by Cravens in 1888 and withdrawn in 1937.*

Above *East of Monymusk station the Alford branch once crossed this lane on a bridge. All that remains are the stone abutments on either side. Monymusk station, located a mile from the village it once served, is now a private residence.*

ceased on 2 January 1950. Despite this, freight continued to be carried on the line until 3 January 1966 when the section from Paradise Siding, between Kintore and Kemnay, and Alford closed completely. Traffic from the quarry at Paradise Siding to Kintore continued until 7 November that year when it too was closed. Kintore station on the Aberdeen to Inverness main line was closed in 1964 although there are now plans to reopen it.

THE LINE TODAY

OS LANDRANGER MAPS NOS. 37 & 38

Today, the first three miles of the trackbed of the Alford branch to the west of Kintore is now used by heavy lorries transporting granite from a large quarry near Kemnay. The quarry was once rail-connected until closure of this section of the line in 1966 and reinstatement of the railway to the quarry would make a lot of environmental sense!

In Kemnay, new housing and roads have obliterated all traces of the railway but to the west of the village low embankments, cuttings and the remains of small bridges can be seen at various locations alongside the B993 as far as Tillyfourie. Located a mile from the village that it once served, Monymusk station building is now a private residence.

West of Tillyfourie the route of the line disappears into the coniferous woodland that once supplied traffic for the railway. The last three miles of the line to Alford runs alongside the A944 where isolated bridge abutments now stand surrounded by ploughed fields.

The scene today at Alford has completely changed. Here the 2ft gauge Alford Valley Railway runs trains to Haughton Country Park using equipment saved from a closed peat railway at New Pitsligo. The original GNoSR engine shed and platform have survived, the former has been recently restored and is used for stabling stock. The former turntable pit is now a flower bed. A new wooden station building has been built on the platform by volunteers and this now houses a small museum and tourist information centre. For more information about the railway visit: www.alfordvalleyrailway.org.uk

Also in Alford is the excellent Grampian Transport Museum (www.gtm.org.uk).

Left *Another view of the enthusiasts special at Monymusk on 13 June 1960. The train was well equipped with preserved wooden carriages and an ex-LNER caféteria coach. The smartly dressed guard is probably on his way to round up any stragglers goggling at the old coach body on the opposite platform.*

Above *Although the embankment on the left of this former bridge has disappeared beneath a ploughed field, these two stone bridge abutments mark the route of the line where it once crossed a lane two miles east of Alford.*

Right *LNER days – the branch train to Kintore waits to depart from quiet Alford station on a summer day in 1936. The locomotive is ex-GNoSR Class O (LNER Class D42) 4-4-0 No. 6817.*

Left *Things aren't quite what they appear at Alford station today. While the platform is still the original structure, the wooden station building of the 2ft gauge Alford Valley Railway was built by volunteers. In the distance the original engine shed has been restored to its former glory. The railway runs passenger services to Haughton Park between April and September.*

Right *Today the turntable pit at Alford has become a flower bed but keen eyes will spot the granite buffer stops that can be seen in the old photograph below.*

Above *A busy scene at Alford station in the early 20th century. The platform is thronged with passengers just having disembarked from their train, while in the station yard are several Great North of Scotland Railway charabancs. The GNoSR operated a large number of these vehicles as feeder services to carry passengers from railway stations to outlying villages and beauty spots. In the foreground is the small turntable that enabled the GNoSR 4-4-0 tender locomotives to turn before returning down the line to Alford.*

HAUGHTON PARK
HAUGHTON PARK

Above *Alford station came to life on 13 June 1960 when an enthusiasts special visited the branch line. The old Wolseley and Sunbeam Rapier would not go amiss in today's Grampian Transport Museum which can also be found in Alford.*

Left *A delicate manoeuvre as Alford Valley Railway carriages are reversed into the restored engine shed at Alford. Some of the stock used on this 2ft gauge line originally came from a peat line at New Pitsligo.*

Right *BR Standard Class 2 2-6-0 No. 78045 gets ready to leave Alford with the daily freight for Kintore in July 1961. It wasn't long before these steam locomotives were replaced by North British Locomotive Company Type 2 diesels based at Aberdeen Kittybrewster shed, although their reign was a short one due to their appalling reliability record.*

DINGWALL and STRATHPEFFER.—Highland.

Miles	Week Days only.	mrn	mrn	mrn	aft	aft	aft
	Dingwall..........dep.	8 30	10 5	11 20	2 0	4 30	6 15
5	Strathpeffer..........arr.	8 40	10 15	11 30	2 10	4 40	6 25

Miles	Week Days only.	mrn	mrn	aft	aft	aft	aft
	Strathpeffer..........dep.	9 0	10 55	1 10	3 20	5 10	6 35
5	Dingwall 870, 871.......arr.	9 10	11 5	1 20	3 30	5 20	6 45

DINGWALL TO STRATHPEFFER

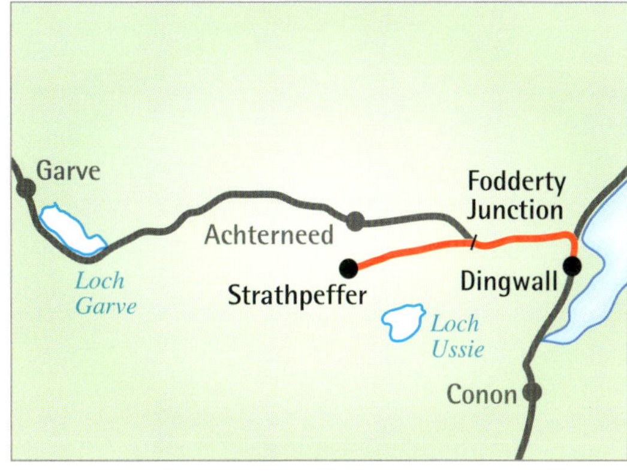

Left *Strathpeffer station and its ornate canopy have been restored to their former glory and now house craft shops, a café and museum. If local landowners hadn't been so obstructive in the 1860s this station would today be served by trains to Kyle of Lochalsh.*

Below *Dingwall station during Highland Railway days in 1913. Nearly 100 years later the station remains basically unchanged. The bay platform for the Strathpeffer branch was located at the far end of the northbound platform just past the road overbridge.*

The first part of the Highland Railway's route from Inverness to Wick and Thurso was opened as far as Dingwall in 1862. Construction pushed northward, linking up with the Duke of Sutherland's railway between Dunrobin and Helmsdale, eventually creating a circuitous route by 1874.

In the meantime the 63-mile Dingwall & Skye Railway had been authorised in 1865 to be built through sparsely populated and remote terrain to Kyle of Lochalsh on the west coast. Supported by the Highland Railway and the Caledonian Railway, the planned route of the new railway would have taken it through the up-and-coming health spa resort of Strathpeffer, but, despite the obvious economic attraction of the railway serving the village, several local landowners objected to the line being built through their land. The problem was eventually overcome by building the new railway north of Strathpeffer via the steeply graded Ravens Rock Summit. The new railway, with a station for Strathpeffer located two miles from the village it served, was opened in 1870.

Left *Ex-Caledonian Railway Pickersgill Class 3P 4-4-0 No. 54487 gets ready for a day's work at Dingwall engine shed on 17 June 1960. The loco was withdrawn when just over 40 years old in March 1961 and the engine shed was closed in December 1961. The same locomotive, albeit with its old LMS number, features in the photograph below.*

Below *Carrying its new British Railways lettering on the tender but still with the old LMS number on the cab, ex-Caledonian Railway Pickersgill Class 3P 4-4-0 No. 14487 trundles through Dingwall station on 15 June 1949. Built by Armstrong Whitworth in 1921 this loco was withdrawn from Inverness shed (60A) in March 1961.*

The people of Strathpeffer were soon to regret the routing of the new railway away from their village. Its growing popularity as a spa resort soon led to demands for a branch line from Dingwall to serve the village. The new railway, authorised in 1884 with half of its five-mile route following the Kyle line from Dingwall as far as Fodderty Junction, was opened by the Highland Railway to Strathpeffer on 3 June 1885. The original Strathpeffer station on the Kyle line was then renamed Achterneed. Passenger trains, hauled by diminutive Highland Railway tank locomotives, often carrying the name 'Strathpeffer', amounted to six return journeys each weekday. A Sentinel steam railcar – known affectionately as 'Chip Vans' – was also used on the branch in the late 1920s.

The Strathpeffer branch was an early victim of rail closures after World War II – passenger services ceased on 23 February 1946 with freight services lasting until 26 March 1951. If the route of the Kyle line had been built as originally planned then Strathpeffer would still be served by a railway today.

THE LINE TODAY

OS Landranger Map No. 26

Dingwall station is still served by trains from Inverness to Kyle of Lochalsh, Wick and Thurso. The Strathpeffer bay at the north end of Dingwall station is now overgrown since closure to passengers in 1946. However, the route of the branch line as it crosses farmland from Fodderty Junction on the Kyle line can be seen from the A834 while the final mile into Strathpeffer is now a footpath which starts next to a water treatment works to the east of the village. The station at Strathpeffer has been restored, complete with original ornate canopy and platform, and now houses craft shops, a café and the Highland Museum of Childhood. The latter houses a doll's collection, doll's houses, toys and photographs and is open from April to the end of October. For more details visit: www.highlandmuseumofchildhood.org.uk

Above *Sixty-five years after the Strathpeffer branch closed to passengers the bay at the north end of Dingwall station is now hidden by undergrowth.*

Above and right *While most of the short Strathpeffer branch from Fodderty Junction now runs through farmland, the last mile into the village is a footpath and muddy track. The path starts (above) next to the water treatment works which is approached up a track from the A834 to the east of Strathpeffer and ends (right) on the final approach to the restored station.*

14898

Above *A view of Strathpeffer station in 1913 by which time the residents of the health resort village were regretting their obstruction nearly 50 years earlier when the Dingwall & Skye Railway was forced to build its line two miles away to the north.*

Left *Pretty as a picture – ex-Highland Railway 'Ben' Class 4-4-0 No. 14398 'Ben Alder' is seen running round its train at Strathpeffer on 18 May 1928. The loco was later scheduled for preservation by British Railways but was mysteriously scrapped after being stored for years at various locations around Scotland. In the distance is Sentinel steam railcar No. 4149.*

Above *A mixed train awaits to depart from Strathpeffer station for Dingwall in 1937. With World War Two looming, the end was in sight for passenger services on the LMS branch which ceased in February 1946 while freight continued until March 1951.*

Above and right *Once a popular destination for health-conscious Victorians wishing to drink the waters of local sulphurous springs, the wooden station building, ornate canopy and platform at Strathpeffer now house craft shops, an information centre, café and the Highland Museum of Childhood.*

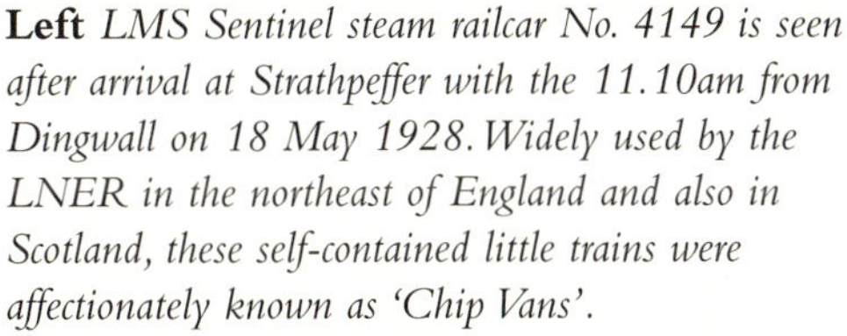

Left *LMS Sentinel steam railcar No. 4149 is seen after arrival at Strathpeffer with the 11.10am from Dingwall on 18 May 1928. Widely used by the LNER in the northeast of England and also in Scotland, these self-contained little trains were affectionately known as 'Chip Vans'.*

DORNOCH and THE MOUND.—Highland.

Miles		Week Days only. mrn		aft		aft			
	Dornoch ....dep.	1055	....	1 5	....	4 40	....	....	....
2¼	Embo	11 2	....	1 13	....	4 51	....	....	....
4	Skelbo	11 9	....	1 20	....	5 1	....	....	....
6½	Cambusavie Platform..	f	....	f	....	f	....	....	....
7¾	The Mound 870 .. arr.	1120	....	1 31	....	5 15	....	....	....

Miles		Week Days only. mrn		aft		aft		
	The Mound ....dep.	1140	....	2 0	....	6 43	....	....
1¼	Cambusavie Platform..	f	....	f	....	f	....	....
3¾	Skelbo	1154	....	2 11	....	6 57	....	....
5½	Embo	12 4	....	2 18	....	7 7	....	....
7¾	Dornoch ....arr.	1212	....	2 26	....	7 15	....	....

f Stop when required.

THE MOUND TO DORNOCH

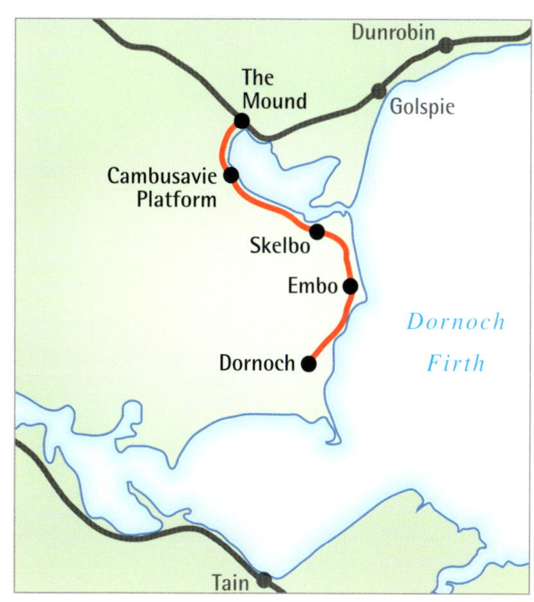

Although the Highland Railway's meandering line from Inverness to the far north had reached Golspie by 13 April 1868, the county town of Dornoch was still seven miles from the nearest station at The Mound. For many years the townsfolk of Dornoch had to make do with a coach service to connect with trains at this station but by the late 19th century there were growing demands from local businessmen for a railway to serve their town.

The passing of the Light Railways Act in 1896 was a turning point for many new rural railways around the UK, enabling them to be built to less exacting standards than other lines and in turn reducing construction costs. Following hot on the heels of this Act coming into force the Dornoch Light Railway Company was formed to build a 7¾-mile line from the town to The Mound.

Left *Between Skelbo and Cambusavie Platform the Dornoch branch skirted the shore of Loch Fleet, where large numbers of seals can often be seen basking on sand banks. This platelayers' hut is a surprising survivor of the railway.*

Below *'Black Five' 4-6-0 No. 45479 pauses at The Mound with the 8.25am Wick to Inverness train on 23 April 1952 while the single-coach Dornoch branch train awaits its loco on the right. The 'blood and custard' coaches of this period were particularly attractive.*

Above *Until the introduction of two Western Region pannier tanks in 1957 the regular branch locos were ex-Highland Railway 0-4-4s Nos. 55051 and 55053. Here, the former loco sporting its new BR livery waits to depart from The Mound with the 11.55am train to Dornoch on 23 April 1952.*

Below *Hundreds of miles from home BR-built Western Region 0-6-0 pannier tank No. 1646 waits to depart from The Mound with its mixed train for Dornoch on 10 September 1959. Following closure of the Dornoch branch in 1960 this loco languished in Scotland until withdrawal at the end of 1962.*

The chairman was the Duke of Sutherland who had already been instrumental in the building of the Far North line between Golspie and Helmsdale – he contributed land and finance to assist in the building of the Dornoch line which also received a government grant towards its construction. The line was authorised in 1898 although many restrictions were imposed including a 25mph speed limit, line-side fencing and level-crossing gates. The main engineering feature on the line was a causeway and viaduct across Loch Fleet near The Mound – the causeway was originally built with a road along the top to replace a ferry across the loch in 1816.

Worked from the outset by the Highland Railway, the Dornoch Light Railway opened amid great rejoicing in the town on 2 June 1902. With intermediate stations at Embo, Skelbo and Cambusavie, train services eventually settled down to three return trips each weekday. Goods traffic, including fish from Embo, was carried with the passenger service which ran as a mixed train. As one of the main sponsors of the railway, the Duke of Sutherland also had the right to run his own train over the line providing sufficient notice was given. Still open for business today, the Dornoch Hotel was opened by the Highland Railway shortly after the opening of the line.

The first locomotive to operate the branch was 0-6-0 tank 'Dornoch' which was designed by William Stroudley and built at the Highland Railway's Loch Gorm Works. This loco was the forerunner of Stroudley's 'Terrier' locomotives later built for the London Brighton and South Coast Railway. From 1905 the line was operated by diminutive Highland Railway tank locomotives (BR Nos. 55051/55053) until they were withdrawn in 1957. The last three years on the Dornoch branch saw 'foreigners' drafted in from the Western Region in the form of Class '1600' pannier tanks Nos. 1646 and 1649. Most passenger trains featured goods wagons while the guard also had to open the several level-crossing gates along the line. Needless to say progress along the line was decidedly slow!

Although worked by the Highland Railway from its opening, the Dornoch Light Railway

Right *Originally built in 1816, the causeway across Loch Fleet from The Mound was also used by Dornoch branch trains when the line opened in 1902. It now carries the much improved A9 trunk road.*

remained independent until 1923 when it became part of the mighty LMS. The little line survived longer than many other Scottish branch lines that were swept away after World War II but the end came on 13 June 1960 when both goods and passenger services ceased. The rusting rails remained in place for another two years until they were lifted in the summer of 1962.

THE LINE TODAY

OS LANDRANGER MAP NO. 21

Much of the Dornoch branch can be traced today. The Mound station building is now a private residence while the causeway aross Loch Fleet that once carried the railway has been widened as part of improvements to the A9. Between the site of Cambusavie Platform and Skelbo a fine example of a brick platelayers' hut stands next to the minor road that runs along the shore of Loch Fleet. Close to Skelbo Castle, the platform, wooden huts and level-crossing gate posts still survive at the site of Skelbo station. Embo station has not survived but the trackbed south of here towards Dornoch is now a footpath. At the end of the line Dornoch station building and platform survive in a small industrial estate.

Above *Close to The Mound station this bricked-up abutment is all that remains of the bridge that once carried the Dornoch branch to the causeway across Loch Fleet. Although now closed, The Mound station buildings still survive as a private residence.*

Above *Ex-HR 0-4-4 tank No. 55051 approaches The Mound across the causeway over Loch Fleet with the 10.35am train from Dornoch on 23 April 1952. Although the bridge on the left has since been demolished the causeway now carries the A9 trunk road between Wick and Inverness.*

Below *The first station out from The Mound was at Cambusavie where Mrs Kathleen Casserley can be seen posing on the platform during her husband's visit to the Dornoch branch in April 1952. The level-crossing gates on this line were operated by the guard who had to jump off and on the train.*

Below *Near Skelbo Castle, this small stone bridge marks the Dornoch branch line's route alongside the shore of Loch Fleet. The loch, along with the Dornoch Firth, is now a National Nature Reserve designated as a Special Protection Area. Birdlife includes osprey, greylag goose, wigeon, curlew, dunlin and oystercatcher.*

Below *After Cambusavie the next station was at Skelbo where the train's guard can be seen opening the level-crossing gate on 3 June 1960. The mixed branch train behind Western Region 0-6-0 pannier tank No. 1646 waits patiently for the road ahead. What a beautiful summer's day with blue skies and a carpet of wild flowers next to the track – sadly, this scene disappeared only 10 days later when the line closed for good.*

Below *No. 1646 has proceeded on its leisurely journey to Dornoch on 3 June 1960. Here the train has halted at Embo station, once a source of fish traffic for the branch line.*

Above *Skelbo station today – the platform, wooden huts and level-crossing gateposts still survive while the fir tree seen in the two photographs on the left has grown considerably.*

Left *It's all in the detail – at first glance this photograph of Skelbo taken from the 11.55am train to Dornoch on 23 April 1952 shows that little changed in the eight years that followed. However, on closer inspection and comparing it with the 1960 photo we can deduce that the fir tree alongside the track has grown about eight feet during that period!*

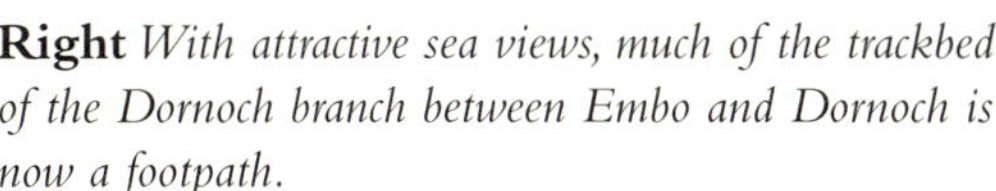

Right *With attractive sea views, much of the trackbed of the Dornoch branch between Embo and Dornoch is now a footpath.*

LIPTONS

Below *Ex-Highland Railway 0-4-4 tank loco carrying its LMS number 15052 waits patiently at Dornoch for three smartly dressed ladies to board the 9am train for The Mound on 19 May 1928. In the distance is the squat spire of Dornoch's 13th-century cathedral.*

Railway travellers in this part of Scotland were (and still are) subjected to travelling great distances to reach destinations that are geographically only a few miles away. The distance from Dornoch to Tain, only five miles across the Dornoch Firth as the crow flies, involved a rail journey to The Mound where passengers changed trains for the journey to Tain via Lairg, a total distance of 44¼ miles. In recent years, improvements to the A9 trunk road have alleviated this problem for motorists. If the promoters of the Dornoch Rail Link have their way, a new railway will be built from Golspie to Tain via Dornoch and a bridge over the Dornoch Firth – what the residents of Lairg will think about that is another matter!

Left *Although operated by the Highland Railway from the outset, the Dornoch Light Railway remained independent until the Big Four Grouping of 1923. The first locomotive to operate the branch was the 0-6-0 tank 'Dornoch', which was designed by William Stroudley and built at the Highland Railway's Loch Gorm Works; it is seen here at Dornoch engine shed soon after opening. It had previously been named 'Fort George' for working on that branch line and was the forerunner of Stroudley's 'Terrier' locomotives later built for the London Brighton and South Coast Railway.*

Below *Not much had changed at Dornoch in the space of 50 years – this view of the single-road engine shed was taken in 1952. At the time, the shed was home to one of the ex-HR 0-4-4 tanks used on the branch. No. 55051 can be seen in the distance waiting to depart with the 1.15pm train for The Mound.*

Above *Newly arrived from the Western Region, 0-6-0 pannier tank No. 1646 waits to depart from Dornoch with a mixed train for The Mound in May 1957. Along with sister engine No. 1649 this loco was 'borrowed' from duties in south Wales when the last Highland Railway 0-4-4 broke a leading axle and was withdrawn. The two WR locos were built at Swindon in 1951 and, after a short working life, were cut up at Cowlairs Works in 1963.*

Right *Dornoch station and platform are still easily recognisable today. The station building is home to a chiropractic clinic while the station site now features industrial units.*

LYBSTER and WICK.—Highland.

Miles.		Week Days only. mrn		aft	aft		
	Lybster .... dep.	7 10	....	1 0	6 15	....	....
1½	Occumster	7 16	....	1 5	6 22	....	....
4	Mid-Clyth	7 24	....	1 14	6 33	....	....
6½	Ulbster	7 32	....	1 21	6 42	....	....
9½	Thrumster	7 40	....	1 30	6 53	....	....
13¾	Wick 870 .... arr.	7 53	....	1 42	7 5	....	....

Miles.		Week Days only. mrn		aft	aft			
	Wick .... dep.	1130	....	4 15	7 20	....	....	...
4¼	Thrumster	1145	....	4 30	7 32	....	....	...
7¼	Ulbster	1156	....	4 41	7 41	....	....	...
9¾	Mid-Clyth	12 5	....	4 50	7 48	....	....	...
12¼	Occumster	1216	....	5 1	7 57	....	....	...
13¾	Lybster .... arr.	1220	....	5 5	8 1	....	....	...

WICK TO LYBSTER

Authorised in 1866, the first railway to Wick, the Caithness Railway from Thurso, was never built due to lack of funds and it was not until 1874 that the meandering Far North line from Inverness had arrived in the town. The line from Helmsdale was forced to take a circuitous inland route instead of following a shorter route due to the difficult terrain along the east coast. In the meantime the coastal fishing villages to the south of Wick, notably Lybster with its new harbour financed by the Duke of Portland, were some miles from their nearest railhead.

As with the Dornoch Light Railway (see pages 132-143), the passing of the Light Railways Act in 1896 transformed the building of railways in sparsely populated parts of the UK. Thanks to financial backing of the Highland Railway, the Duke of Portland and local councils and a £25,000 grant from the government, the Wick & Lybster Light Railway was authorised in 1899 to build a 13½-mile line between these two named places. Worked from the outset by the Highland Railway and with intermediate stations at Thrumster, Ulbster, Mid Clyth and Occumster, the line opened for business on 1 July 1903 but a proposed seven-mile extension to the fishing village of Dunbeath never materialised. Request halts at Welsh's Crossing, Roster Road and Parkside were later opened by the LMS in 1936.

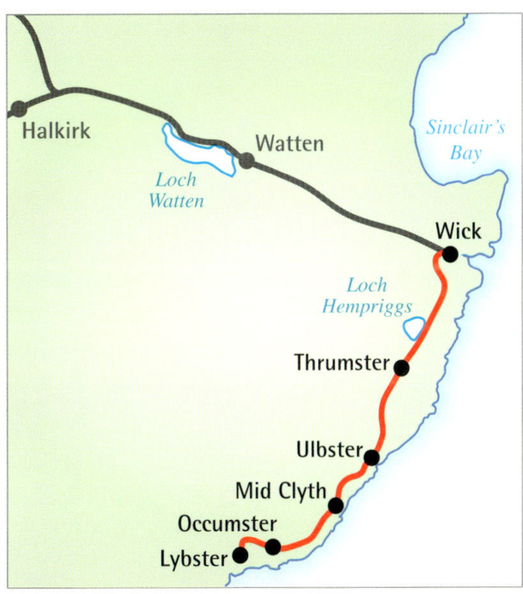

Left *Alongside the A9 four miles south of Wick the wooden station building and platform of Thrumster station have been saved in near original condition. All that is missing is the station clock and a train arriving on the authentically laid length of spiked track.*

Right *The LMS had by far the most track mileage of any of the Big Four railway companies in the UK. Even the Lybster branch wasn't forgotten on this sign at Wick station in 1931*

15050

Left *Ideal for working the lightly laid branch lines to Dornoch and Lybster, the diminutive Highland Railway 0-4-4 tanks were the last locomotive types of this company to remain in revenue-earning service with British Railways. Here, in LMS days, Lybster branch engine No. 15050 simmers outside Wick engine shed on 21 May 1928.*

Above *Stanier 'Black Five' 4-6-0 No. 44783 receives undivided attention from a mother and her small child before departing with a train for Inverness on 9 September 1959. The delivery lorry on the platform has probably brought a fresh catch of fish – still an important source of revenue for the railways at that date – from the harbour for onward despatch by rail. Steam haulage on the Far North line was replaced by diesel power in 1962. Today Class 158 DMUs operate the heavily subsidised route for First ScotRail. Strangely, trains from Georgemas Junction to Wick take 40 minutes for the 14¼-mile journey because they first make a return journey to Thurso!*

Until 1929 the three return mixed trains each weekday were in the hands of a small 0-4-4 tank loco, suitably renamed 'Lybster', that had formerly worked on the Strathpeffer branch (see pages 122–131). On this loco's demise the branch locos were usually 4-4-0 'Yankee' tank No. 15103 or 0-4-4 tanks Nos. 15050 and 15053 (by then all with LMS numbers) – the latter loco also sometimes seeing service on the Dornoch branch – and passengers were conveyed in ancient and uncomfortable six-wheeled gas-lit carriages not deemed fit for use elsewhere on the system.

Passenger traffic was never heavy on the line but it was boosted in 1922 when the townsfolk of Wick voted for the prohibition of alcohol – promoted by the Temperance Movement to halt the alcoholic violence that was then overtaking the town. From that date those wishing to partake of an alcoholic bevvy just hopped on a train to Lybster! The ban remained in place until 28 May 1947. Although the fishing industry at Lybster benefitted greatly from the opening of the railway, traffic on the line never lived up to expectations and by the beginning of World War II its future looked uncertain. The end came with road improvements south of Wick following which the little line was unceremoniously closed on 1 April 1944 and ripped up for scrap to aid the war effort. With an existence of just under 41 years the Wick & Lybster Light Railway had one of the shortest working lives of any railway in Scotland and even in the UK.

THE LINE TODAY

OS Landranger Maps Nos. 11 & 12

Wick station is still open and served by trains from Thurso and Inverness. Closely paralleling the A9 trunk road – improvements to which finally sealed the railway's fate in 1944 – the route of the Wick to Lybster line can easily be traced today. At the northern end the line looped inland to join the 'main line' just to the west of Wick station.

For a light railway that only operated for 41 years there are still a surprising number of significant remains to be seen today. Crossing keepers' cottages, all now in use as private residences, can be found at many locations along the line. However the most intact station is at Thrumster which stands alongside the A9 four miles south of Wick. Complete with platform and a short length of authentically spiked track, the wooden station building is preserved in a remarkable original condition.

Further south, the stone curving platform of Ulbster station lies at the end of a narrow lane that leads to important archaeological sites such as brochs and chambered cairns located near Loch Watenan. Whether the stone railway platform will survive for 2,000 years is unlikely. The base of the wooden passenger shelter can clearly be seen on the platform.

The end of the line is at Lybster and here the former wooden station building, with more modern extensions, is now the clubhouse for Lybster Golf Club. Much of the platform still remains but the engine shed was demolished in 1997 and the goods shed in 2003. Visitors to the station today receive a cheery welcome from the groundsman who still has fond memories of the steam-hauled trains between Wick and Inverness.

Above *729 miles from Euston, Wick station, seen here in July 1931, was the furthest main line outpost of the mighty LMS – Lybster was another 13½ miles further south. Apart from the posters, gas lights and the John Menzies shop not much has changed at Wick over the intervening 80 years.*

Right *Hidden away up a lane that leads to an amazing collection of ancient brochs, chambered cairns and standing stones, the curving stone platform of Ulbster station is a more recent example of archaeological remains. The base of the wooden passenger shelter is clearly visible on the platform.*

Above *Apart from the front door and missing clock, perfectly preserved Thrumster station is in near original condition. Buffeted by gales blowing in from the North Sea, the station, which has stood here since 1903, backs on to the A9 trunk road four miles south of Wick.*

Right *The trackbed of the Lybster branch disappears northwards across bleak farmland between Mid Clyth and Occumster. The landscape in this most northerly part of mainland Scotland is littered with ruined crofts and ancient remains of chambered cairns, brochs and standing stones.*

Left *This small concrete bridge once carried the Lybster branch line over a stream near East Clyth. Following closure of the line in 1944 the rails were hurriedly ripped up to aid the war effort!*

Above *The only sign of life today at the site of Occumster station is this flock of sheep standing on the trackbed of the line. The line continued southwards from here before crossing the A9 and making a final loop down to the terminus at Lybster.*

Below *Ex-Highland Railway 4-4-0 tank No. 15013 waits at Lybster with its train of ancient six-wheeled carriages before departing with the 8.45pm train to Wick on 19 May 1928. This far-flung outpost of the LMS had had a very short working life of just under 41 years when it closed on 1 April 1944.*

The loco featured here was one of five originally built by Dübs & Co of Glasgow for the Uruguay Eastern Railway between 1891 and 1893. The order was cancelled due to financial problems and the locos, subsequently nicknamed 'Yankees', were bought by the Highland Railway for use on branch lines.

15013
LYBSTER
LIPTONS

Below *The tall timber-built single-road engine shed at Lybster was supported on each side as a precaution against easterly gales blowing in from the North Sea. Just out of the picture to the left was a 43ft 6in turntable. Despite closure in 1944 the engine shed survived until 1997 and the goods shed until 2003.*

Above and top right *With a few more recent extensions the wooden station building at Lybster terminus is now the clubhouse for Lybster Golf Club. The line of the platform is clearly visible (top right) while the circular frame for the station clock can be seen on the left. The positioning of the modern white water closet by the front door seems rather suspect!*

Below *Ex-Highland Railway 0-4-4 tank No. 15053 takes on water at remote Lybster engine shed on 18 July 1931. Built as a light railway the track on the Lybster branch was spiked directly onto sleepers, thus avoiding the use of costly cast-iron chairs. Following closure of the Lybster branch in 1944 this loco moved south to work on the Dornoch branch until withdrawn from Helmsdale shed (60C) in January 1957, thus becoming the last HR loco, at the grand old age of 51, to remain in revenue-earning service with BR.*

INDEX

END OF THE LINE – a concrete sleeper graveyard somewhere in Ayrshire.

PHOTOGRAPHIC ACKNOWLEDGEMENTS

All modern-day colour photographs by Julian Holland

t = top; *b* = bottom; *m* = middle; *l* = left; *r* = right

Henry Casserley: 3/4; 19b; 31b; 39; 42/43; 45b; 49b; 50; 58t; 58b; 65t; 66b; 69b; 85t; 86b; 88b; 94b; 102t; 114; 124b; 128/129; 130; 133b; 134t; 136t; 136b; 138b; 140/141; 142b; 145b; 146; 148t; 152/153; 154/155

Richard Casserley: 18t; 20/21; 77ml; 82b; 85b; 97t; 109; 110t; 116; 121t

Colour-Rail: 11b; 15t; 17t; 21b; 22t; 25b; 26t; 29t; 31t; 37b; 67t; 67b; 70t; 82t; 91b; 96b; 101b; 111t; 121b; 124t; 138tl; 139tr; 143t; 147t

John Goss: 1; 10t; 34; 36; 38; 40; 93; 95; 98

Tony Harden: 9b; 13t; 17b; 18b; 25t; 33b; 35b; 43t; 47t; 53t; 60t; 62b; 64t; 66t; 70b; 81b; 86t; 88t; 99b; 102b; 105t; 106b; 113b; 119t; 119b; 123b; 134b; 142t

Bill Jamieson: 72t; 72b

Leadhills & Wanlockhead Railway: 47b; 53b; 54t; 54b

Bruce MacCartney: 75t; 77t; 77br; 79tr

Stuart Sellar: 16/17; 26/27; 74; 76t

Frank Spaven: 13b; 15b; 61

Andrew Swift: 62t